The Great Depression

The History of the Industrialized World

(Stories of Those With Depression and How They Helped Themselves)

Ernesto Brown

Published By **Bengion Cosalas**

Ernesto Brown

All Rights Reserved

The Great Depression: The History of the Industrialized World (Stories of Those With Depression and How They Helped Themselves)

ISBN 978-1-7773611-4-3

No part of this guidebook shall be reproduced in any form without permission in writing from the publisher except in the case of brief quotations embodied in critical articles or reviews.

Legal & Disclaimer

The information contained in this book is not designed to replace or take the place of any form of medicine or professional medical advice. The information in this book has been provided for educational & entertainment purposes only.

The information contained in this book has been compiled from sources deemed reliable, and it is accurate to the best of the Author's knowledge; however, the Author cannot guarantee its accuracy and validity and cannot be held liable for any errors or omissions. Changes are periodically made to this book. You must consult your doctor or get professional medical advice before using any of the suggested remedies, techniques, or information in this book.

Upon using the information contained in this book, you agree to hold harmless the Author from and against any damages, costs, and expenses, including any legal fees potentially resulting from the application of any of the information provided by this guide. This disclaimer applies to any damages or injury caused by the use and application, whether directly or indirectly, of any advice or information presented, whether for breach of contract, tort, negligence, personal injury, criminal intent, or under any other cause of action.

You agree to accept all risks of using the information presented inside this book. You need to consult a professional medical practitioner in order to ensure you are both able and healthy enough to participate in this program.

Table Of Contents

Chapter 1: Great Depression 1

Chapter 2: The 9 Main Impacts Of Depression 24

Chapter 3: Implications Of The Great Depression 37

Chapter 4: The End Of The Great Depression 49

Chapter 5: What Was The Great Depression? 73

Chapter 6: What Triggered The Great Depression? 79

Chapter 7: Nonconformist Ideas About The Depression 90

Chapter 8: The Cause And Effect Of The Depression 97

Chapter 9: How It Impacted Different Nations 108

Chapter 10: Healing From The Great Depression 122

Chapter 11: The Last Rains 132

Chapter 12: A Photograph Of Dirt Piling Up In The Direction Of A Barn In Kansas 144

Chapter 13: A Photograph Of Buried Machinery In Dallas, South Dakota 157

Chapter 14: The Bank Or The Company 172

Chapter 15: The Dust Came In So Thinly 180

Chapter 1: Great Depression

The 1929–1939 Great Depression become a global monetary melancholy that affected all worldwide locations. The industrialized Western worldwide had by no means in advance than confronted a melancholy of such length and severity, and as a give up end result, financial establishments, macroeconomic coverage, and monetary idea underwent splendid modifications. Despite having its roots in the United States, the Great Depression had a profound effect on almost each nation in the globe, important to sharp drops in output, excessive ranges of unemployment, and acute deflation. No less startling were its social and cultural repercussions, specifically in the United States, wherein the Great Depression emerge as america's worst period of trouble for the motive that Civil War.

There had been massive community versions inside the Great Depression's timing and intensity. In evaluation to Japan and components of Latin America, in which it turn out to be milder, the Depression modified into substantially extended and excessive in the United States and Europe. It may additionally furthermore come as no marvel that a range of things contributed to the best monetary downturn the arena has ever identified. The United States financial output declined because of declines in purchaser call for, financial panic, and poorly notion-out authorities policies. The gold cutting-edge, which associated nearly all worldwide locations in the global in a network of consistent foreign exchange fees, changed into critical in spreading the American downturn to important worldwide locations. The elimination of the gold present day and the subsequent financial enlargement were essential people to the Great Depression's recuperation. The Great Depression had a fantastic affect on the economic tool, ensuing in both excessive human distress and large shifts in economic method.

Timing And Severity:

In the summer season of 1929, the USA had a everyday recession in advance than the start of the Great Depression. However, the stoop substantially worsened in late 1929 and endured till early 1933. Real manufacturing and fees each dropped sharply. The United States had a 47 percent fall in commercial production at some degree in the downturn's height and a 30 percentage decline in the actual gross home product (GDP). The index of wholesale expenses fell 33%. (such declines in the price diploma are referred to as deflation). Although there's some confrontation over the validity of the data, it's far usually time-honored that the unemployment price at its pinnacle changed into better than 20%. When in comparison to the Great Recession of 2007–2009, which saw the u . S . A .'s actual GDP decrease with the resource of honestly 4.Three percentage and its unemployment fee attain a top of heaps lots much less than 10 percentage, the Great Depression inside the United States severity is made extra apparent. Almost every state in the globe became impacted by way of the Great Depression. The downturn's timing and severity, but, differed substantially amongst worldwide locations. For maximum of the 1920s 2d half, Great Britain battled with gradual development and recession. However, the us of a did now not input a deep depression until the start of 1930, and the decrease in commercial enterprise manufacturing from its top to its trough turn out to be approximately one-1/three that of the United States. The early Thirties noticed a drastically quick recession in France as well. However, the French comeback in 1932 and 1933 have become certainly brief. Between 1933 and 1936, there was a extensive decline in each French business manufacturing and fees. Early in

1928, Germany's economic gadget commenced out out to agreement earlier than stabilizing and contracting all over again within the zero.33 sector of 1929. German industrial production fell with the aid of way of a comparable quantity to what america skilled. A sort of Latin American nations professional economic downturns in late 1928 and early 1929, a hint bit in advance than the output lower in the United States. While some less advanced countries went via catastrophic depressions, others, like Argentina and Brazil, handiest went via in particular minor recessions. A moderate despair that commenced fairly past due and ended quite early additionally affected Japan.

Other global places skilled the identical massive charge deflation because america. In almost every industrialized u . S . A ., wholesale fees fell with the useful resource of 30% or greater amongst 1929 and 1933. The prolonged flexibility of the Japanese price device brought about a really quick deflation in Japan in 1930 and 1931. This brief deflation may additionally additionally moreover have contributed to the distinctly modest drop in Japanese manufacturing. During this time, the charges of simple commodities traded on worldwide markets fell even extra sharply. For instance, amongst September 1929 and December 1930, the charges of espresso, cotton, silk, and rubber were all cut thru almost half of of. The phrases of exchange for manufacturers of primary commodities appreciably decreased as a forestall result.

In the spring of 1933, the us started out out to get better. Midway thru the Thirties, output surged fast: from 1933 and 1937, real GDP expanded at a mean price of nine% yearly. However, due to how extensively output had plummeted inside the early Nineteen Thirties, it became well underneath its long-run fashion line inside the route of this time. The American economic device saw a few other extreme dip in 1937–1938, however from mid–1938, it extended even more fast than it had within the mid–the Nineteen Thirties. In 1942, the dominion's output at prolonged very last resumed its lengthy-term fashion route. The the relaxation of the sector noticed a reasonably choppy restoration. Although a true healing did not start till the end of 1932, the British economic system stopped shrinking all at once after Great Britain abandoned the gold current in September 1931. In past due 1931 and early 1932, a number of Latin American worldwide places' economies commenced to grow. In the autumn of 1932, every Japan and Germany commenced to get higher. Beginning in early 1933, Canada and severa smaller European worldwide locations commenced to look monetary boom at in the course of the equal time due to the fact the United States. France, but, did not in fact enter the restoration section till 1938, no matter experiencing a extreme droop later than maximum extraordinary global places.

THE CAUSES OF THE DEPRESSION

The primary reason stress of the Great Depression inside the United States emerge as a drop in consumer spending, often called aggregate call for. This decline in call for delivered on a decline in output because of manufacturers and shops observing an unplanned boom in inventories. Over the path of the Depression, the origins of the reduce charge in American spending numerous, but all of them added as a whole lot as a huge drop in combination name for. The gold preferred carried out a awesome function in spreading the American slide to the rest of the globe. But some of different reasons also had a characteristic within the droop in extremely good countries.

Stock Market Collapse

It is usually common that america' strict financial coverage, which grow to be supposed to reduce inventory marketplace speculation, have become the number one purpose of the primary decrease in output at some point of the summer season of 1929. The Twenties had been a a fulfillment decade, however they were no longer a mainly increase time every; prices have been basically strong at some point of the route of the last decade, and 1924 and 1927 each observed slight recessions. The inventory marketplace turn out to be the remarkable blatantly excessive region. Between the low detail in 1921 and the excessive in 1929, inventory values had extended via more than four times. The Federal Reserve improved hobby fees in 1928 and 1929 for you to moderate the pointy boom in stock values. Due to the lower call for for hobby-sensitive spending in industries like creation and car profits, manufacturing fell because of the superior hobby expenses. According to 3 teachers, a residence introduction growth in the mid-Nineteen Twenties led to an oversupply of housing and a pointy decline in development in 1928 and 1929. By the fall of 1929, U.S. Inventory values had risen to heights that weren't supported through sensible earnings projections. Investors misplaced faith therefore, and the stock marketplace bubble burst in October 1929 because of a number of unimportant occurrences that introduced about constant fee reductions. On "Black Thursday," October 24, 1929, panic selling started out out. Many equities have been sold on margin, or with loans that had been high-quality in part backed with the useful resource of the price of the stocks. As a give up end result, numerous shoppers have been obliged to sell their shares due to the rate losses, which increased the lower in costs. U.S. Stock values, as decided thru the Cowles Index, fell 33% among their pinnacle in September and their trough in November. This occurrence is on occasion referred to as the Great Crash of 1929 due to how drastically the autumn took place.

The disintegrate of the inventory marketplace notably decreased American combination call for. Following the crisis, each organisation investment and patron purchases of durable gadgets declined precipitously. The monetary disaster definitely prompted a outstanding deal of uncertainty about future earnings, which in flip brought on human beings and businesses to postpone attempting to find long lasting gadgets. Although there has been now not a great loss of wealth because of the decrease in stock prices, the catastrophe also can have reduced spending via making people experience poorer (see customer self assure). Real output in the United States declined fast in overdue 1929 and into 1930 as a result of the sharp lower in client and business enterprise expenditure, which had been dropping grade by grade up to this point. The decrease in stock prices have become one of the elements main to losses in output and employment in the United States, even though the Great Crash of the inventory marketplace and the Great Depression had been pretty unique occurrences.

Bank panics and economic contractions – Bank holiday within the route of the Great Depression

The 2d blow to traditional call for got here in the form of the primary of 4 waves of economic panic that engulfed america inside the fall of 1930. When numerous depositors concurrently start to doubt the viability of banks and request cash payments for his or her economic institution financial savings, a banking panic effects. Banks need to promote loans a very good way to generate the necessary coins because of the reality they commonly handiest maintain a small a part of deposits as coins reserves. Even a financial institution that had been profitable in advance than going through this moved quick liquidation way may fail. In the autumn of 1930, the spring of 1931, the autumn of 1931, and the autumn of 1932, america found huge monetary panics. The very last wave of panic persisted inside the path of the winter of 1933 and ended on March 6, 1933, whilst President Franklin D. Roosevelt proclaimed a national "monetary organization tour." All banks have been closed for the economic group excursion, and satisfactory folks that authorities inspectors determined to be solvent have been allowed to reopen. The American financial system have turn out to be seriously damaged with the resource of manner of the panics. One-5th of the banks that have been strolling on the start of 1930 had collapsed by way of the twelve months 1933. By their very nature, monetary panics are unpredictable, illogical phenomena, even though some of the causes are understandable. According to financial historians, the 1920s observed big rises in agricultural debt, together with U.S. Policies that supported tiny, undiversified banks, which helped to foster an environment wherein such panics would possibly begin and spread. The immoderate prices of agricultural merchandise in the end of World War I, which endorsed massive borrowing via American farmers hoping to increase production through way of making an funding in land and machinery, had been a contributing detail to the big farm debt. Following the struggle, agricultural commodity costs fell, making it difficult for farmers to make loan payments.

Little turned into completed through the Federal Reserve to try to prevent the banking panics. In their seminal art work A Monetary History of the united states, 1867-1960 (1963), economists Milton Friedman and Anna J. Schwartz contended that the lack of life in 1928 of Benjamin Strong, the governor of the Federal Reserve Bank of New York thinking about that 1914, changed right into a critical element on this inactivity. Strong were a sturdy leader who found how the relevant financial institution need to save you panic. His passing created a strength vacuum on the Federal Reserve, which gave different leaders room to prevent prudent intervention. The panics delivered approximately a pointy increase in humans's choice to hold extra money than that that they had in financial agency deposits. This growth within the foreign exchange-to-deposit ratio come to be a number one issue within the United States declining coins deliver of 31% amongst 1929 and 1933. In September 1931, on the identical time as Britain have come to be forced off the gold big and investors feared that the united states should comply with fit, the Federal Reserve no longer only allow the panics lessen the U.S. Cash supply but furthermore purposefully reduced it and extended hobby prices.

Income and Production In The Us

According to students, the Federal Reserve's alternatives that produced such decreases within the coins supply drastically decreased manufacturing. The first-class example of the critical function monetary disintegrate done in the American Great Depression may be determined in a honest picture. The coins deliver and real output from 1900 to 1945 are depicted within the graph. During common durations, like the Nineteen Twenties, every the cash supply and production have a propensity to growth constantly. But each declined within the early Nineteen Thirties. Numerous elements reduced expenditure at the same time as the cash supply shrank. Most importantly, clients and organizations began to anticipate deflation, that is, they expected destiny salaries and prices to be decrease, as a result of actual charge drops and the fast decline inside the money supply. People have been consequently reluctant to borrow despite the fact that nominal hobby fees were fantastically low because of the fact they were involved that their destiny profits and earnings might also need to no longer be enough to pay decrease back their loans. This hesitation in turn delivered on significant decreases in each patron and agency funding. The panics clearly made the decrease in spending worse with the aid of instilling cynicism and a lack of self warranty. Furthermore, lending turned into interrupted through using the economic wreck of such a whole lot of banks, lowering the quantity of coins available to finance investments.

Benchmark – The Gold Standard

Some economists assume that the Federal Reserve ordinary or sparked the dramatic drops in the US money deliver that permits you to keep america on the gold preferred. To maintain the regular rate under the gold contemporary, each state installed the charge of its foreign exchange in terms of gold and took monetary motion to achieve this. Foreigners might also have out of place faith within the United States adherence to the gold famous if the Federal Reserve had significantly improved the coins deliver in reaction to the banking panics. The United

States might also had been obliged to devalue as a quit end result, which might likely have brought on huge gold outflows. A speculative assault on the greenback may additionally moreover have happened and the US and Great Britain might also furthermore had been pressured to give up the gold preferred if the Federal Reserve had now not limited the money deliver in the fall of 1931.

There is confrontation over the gold full-size's contribution to constraining American monetary policy, however there's no denying that it had a extensive element in spreading america' monetary downturn to the rest of the globe. International gold flows below the gold modern-day had been due to trade or asset waft imbalances. For instance, inside the center of the 1920s, the United States had sizeable inflows of gold due to the first-rate distant places name for for American assets like stocks and bonds. Similarly, France's desire to move once more to the gold elegant after World War I and rent a devalued franc led to alternate surpluses and extraordinary gold inflows. (See additionally alternate stability.)

Following World War I, Britain made the selection to reinstate the gold popular at the prewar parity. However, wartime inflation suggested that the pound modified into overestimated, and after 1925, this overvaluation added on good sized gold outflows and exchange deficits. The Bank of England substantially increased hobby expenses if you want to forestall the flow of gold. Throughout the second part of the Twenties, immoderate-hobby charges decreased British expenditure and contributed to a excessive unemployment price in Great Britain.

The fashion for gold to migrate out of diverse worldwide locations and in the route of the us multiplied after the U.S. Economic gadget started out to go through appreciably. This occurred because of the usa deflation making American objects greater appealing to global purchasers, while American clients' low-profits tiers decreased their choice for foreign places items. Central banks all over the globe extended interest charges to counterbalance the tendency inside the route of an American alternate surplus and remote places gold outflows that resulted. In essence, keeping the worldwide gold well-known wanted a super global financial contraction to wholesome the simplest going on in the US. The very last results changed into a decrease in output and prices around the sector that came near matching the autumn inside the US.

In addition to america, numerous unique countries had financial crises and banking panics. Payment problems at the Creditanstalt, the largest financial institution in Austria, in May 1931 sparked a chain of monetary crises that engulfed a whole lot of Europe and completed a big position in persuading Britain to stop the gold elegant. Austria, Germany, and Hungary have been the diverse global locations that were critically impacted through way of using monetary business enterprise collapses and erratic monetary markets. These excessive economic crises also can had been added on via insufficient regulation, additional neighborhood times, or honest worldwide contagion. Additionally, the gold considerable decreased the price of financial institution collateral and extended their vulnerability to bank runs via requiring certainly one of a type nations to deflate at the equal price because america. Banking panics and other monetary marketplace disturbances, similar to those in the United States, in addition decreased output and expenses in a number of international locations.

International Trade And Lending

Some instructors emphasize the significance of numerous international connections.

Midway through the Nineteen Twenties, remote places financing to Germany and Latin America had drastically elevated, however due to immoderate-hobby charges and a flourishing stock marketplace at domestic, U.S. Lending remote places decreased in 1928 and 1929. It's possible that this lower in foreign places lending contributed to next credit score score contractions and production decreases inside the borrowing international locations. The financial authorities might also were hesitant to put into impact an expansionary insurance to combat the financial downturn in Germany, in which quite speedy inflation (hyperinflation) came about within the early Nineteen Twenties, for fear that it may re-light inflation. The reasons why the economies of Germany, Argentina, and Brazil declined in advance than the begin of the Great Depression within the United States can be associated with the outcomes of decreasing foreign loans. Other troubles were introduced about with the resource of the Smoot-Hawley Tariff Act, which became handed in the United States in 1930, and the global boom of change protectionist measures. In order to increase farm incomes, the Smoot-Hawley tariff decreased foreign places opposition in agricultural merchandise. However, other global places imitated them in retaliation and that allows you to pressure them to deal with their alternate imbalances. Scholars now keep that whilst these guidelines might probably have slightly reduced change, they did no longer notably make contributions to the Depression some of the most enterprise producers. However, protectionist rules may additionally additionally additionally have contributed to the pointy decrease inside the rate of uncooked property, which generated excessive balance of bills issues for worldwide locations in Africa, Asia, and Latin America that produce easy commodities and ended in contractionary monetary and monetary recommendations.

Chapter 2: The 9 Main Impacts Of Depression

How This Dark Period in American History Still Affects You Today, the primary ramifications of FDR's election in 1932 due to the overall public's waning consider in Hoover's laissez-faire economics. During the first 5 years, the GDP collapsed thru 50%, bankrupting businesses. In the Nineteen Thirties, Hoovervilles, or shantytowns, sprouted up in about 6,000 locations. As investment for World War Two accelerated, the Depression led to 1939, giving upward push to the idea that assisting the army permits the financial system. A pure free market economic gadget modified into changed via a blended economic system because of the New Deal and World War II spending. The FDIC turn out to be installed to defend customers. For 25 years, the stock marketplace struggled to get better after dropping ninety% of its price. Until 1941, the unemployment fee have become more than 10%. The gold today's turned into amended via FDR to hold the rate of the greenback, paving the diploma for Nixon to completely abolish it in 1973. The U.S. Financial machine became appreciably broken with the beneficial aid of the Great Depression in 1929. All banks collapsed by way of way of 1-1/3. 1 Homelessness soared, and unemployment advanced to 20-5%. Housing costs fell, trade on a global scale failed, and deflation shot up. The inventory marketplace's recuperation took 25 years.

Although the Great Depression had a large terrible impact on the United States, some outstanding effects emerged from it. For instance, the New Deal obligations installed region measures to lessen the hazard of every other Depression.

The 9 fundamental sectors of the American economic machine that the Great Depression most significantly affected are indexed underneath:

Gross Domestic Product and the financial gadget (GDP)

The economic device dropped through way of 50% in the first five years of the downturn. The gross home product (GDP) indicated that $a hundred and 5 billion modified into the monetary output in 1929. (GDP). That is greater than $1 trillion in present day cash. The financial device started out to agreement in August 1929. One-1/three of all banks had collapsed in advance than the surrender of the twelve months. 1 According to the Bureau of Economic Analysis, the monetary system reduced in size thru way of 8.5% in 1930. (BEA). In 1931 and 1932, the GDP grew by using the use of 6.Four% and 12.Nine%, respectively. The u . S . A . Skilled an monetary downturn for at the least 4 years with the aid of using 1933. It best generated $fifty seven.2 billion, which is set half of of of what it did in 1929. Deflation contributed to a number of the declines. The Consumer

Price Index (CPI), it sincerely is used as a gauge of inflation, reduced via 25% amongst 1929 and 1933, in line with the Bureau of Labor Statistics (BLS). Many corporations went bankrupt because of falling pricing.

Note:

According to the BLS, the unemployment rate reached a immoderate of 24.Nine% in 1933.

In 1934, costs from the New Deal multiplied GDP increase with the aid of way of 10.Eight%. Another 8.Nine% modified into brought in 1935, followed through 12.Nine% in 1936 and 5.1% in 1937. The financial device shrank through three.Three% and the unemployment rate rose to 19% in 1938 because of the authorities reducing decrease decrease again on New Deal costs and the depression returning.

Growth increased thru 8.Eight% in 1940 because of World War II preparations, after developing through the use of 8% in 1939.

The United States entered World War II after Japan struck Pearl Harbor the following 12 months. GDP growth extended every year via 17.7%.

The monetary device modified from being a herbal loose marketplace to a combined financial gadget because of the New Deal and fees for World War II. Its achievement have grow to be in huge component dependent on government expenditure. The Great Depression timeline demonstrates that this modified into a slow—but important—approach.

Politics

The Depression had an effect on politics via manner of undermining manual for unrestrained capitalism. President Herbert Hoover promoted the laissez-faire financial device, and it failed.

People selected President Franklin D. Roosevelt for this reason (FDR). With the assist of government expenditure,

Keynesian economics promised to surrender the Great Depression. The New Deal succeeded. The financial machine progressed and unemployment charges reduced in 1934. FDR, although, started out out to worry approximately such as to the countrywide debt. The national debt come to be $22.5 billion in 1933 and $27 billion in 1934. By 1938, he had reduced authorities spending, and the Depression had yet again.

Nobody desires to devote that errors another time. Politicians now often turn to expansionary economic coverage, which incorporates tax cuts, deficit spending, and special measures. As a quit end result, the country wide debt of the united states has reached a totally immoderate degree. As government expenditure expanded for World War II closer to the stop of the Thirties and the start of the 1940s, the Depression got here to a quit. The assumption that military expenditure is beneficial to the economic device have become born out of this change in spending. Since then, despite the fact that, the government and economists have placed that spending at the army is not the super manner to generate jobs.

Social

Midwest agriculture come to be ravaged thru the Dust Bowl drought. For most farmers, ten years modified into too much time to bear. Even worse, farm commodity prices fell to extremely low stages. Farmers misplaced their houses after they moved in pursuit of employment. Numerous heaps of penniless human beings congregated in "cardboard shacks" called Hoovervilles.

Prohibition changed into resulted in 1933. Due to the sale of now-crook alcohol being taxed, the authorities have become succesful to perform that. FDR implemented the rate variety to help in investment the New Deal.

Because of ways bad it modified into and the manner lengthy it lasted, many humans believed that the American Dream—the notion of being able to pursue one's personal definition of happiness—had come to an prevent. Instead, it altered that fable through such as a claim to monetary blessings.

Unemployment

The unemployment charge have become four.2% in 1928, the final yr of the Roaring Twenties. That is lower than the herbal unemployment charge. It extra than quadrupled to eight.7% with the useful resource of 1930. It had grown to 23.6% via 1932. It rose to a high of virtually 25% in 1933. There had been approximately 15 million unemployed human beings. The unemployment price at that point emerge as the very first-rate ever stated in America. The unemployment charge changed into delivered right right down to 21.7% in 1934, 20.1% in 1935, sixteen.Nine% in 1936, and

14. Three% in 1937 way to New Deal measures. However, in 1938, an entire lot a lot much less lively government expenditure brought on unemployment to upward push as soon as similarly to 19%. Looking at the unemployment fee consistent with one year, you may see that it stayed over 10% till 1941.

Banking

A 0.33 of the us's banks collapsed in some unspecified time in the future of the Great Depression.

Four thousand banks had collapsed with the resource of manner of 1933. The final outcomes become a $140 billion loss for depositors. People have been greatly surprised to have a have a look at that banks had invested within the stock marketplace the use of their financial financial financial savings. Before it have become too past due, they moved fast to withdraw their coins. Even reliable banks had been pushed out of enterprise organization with the beneficial useful resource of these "runs." Fortunately, that now not happens very often. The Federal Deposit Insurance Corporation offers safety for phrase depositors (FDIC). During the New Deal, FDR established this kind of software.

Stock Exchange

90% of the charge of the stock market modified into misplaced amongst 1929 and 1932. It took 25 years for it to get higher. People now not have any religion inside the Wall Street markets. Banks, groups, and individual buyers all went bankrupt. Even non-buyers suffered losses. The fee range from their financial financial savings money owed have been invested thru their banks.

Trade

Countries built change barriers to guard domestic organisation at the same time as their economies deteriorated. In an try to hold American jobs, Congress imposed the Smoot-Hawley price lists in 1930. Other international locations replied in type. As a cease result, change currencies and country wide alliances were used to form shopping for and promoting blocs. Between 1929 and 1934, global alternate fell through 66% (measured in dollars). 20 It had now not but reached its 1929 degree via manner of 1939. Between 1929 and 1932, imports from Europe fell sharply, from $1.Three billion at the outset of the Depression to truly $390 million. Additionally, in the course of that same duration, exports to Europe reduced from $2.Three billion to $784 million.

Deflation

Between 1930 and 1932, fees decreased through the use of 30%.

22 Because mortgage payments hadn't reduced with the useful useful resource of 30%, deflation impacted farmers, groups,

and homeowners more than it harm customers whose income had reduced. As a stop result, many people had mortgage defaults. Homeowners who misplaced the entirety became migratory employees who sought employment wherever they will.

The CPI is shown below as an annual percentage trade.

1929: 0.Zero%

1930: -2.7%

1931: -8.Nine%

1932: -10.3%

1933: -five.2%

1934: three.Five%

1935: 2.6%

1936: 1.Zero%

1937: 3.7%

1938: -2.Zero%

1939: 1.Three%

1940: zero.7%

1941: five.1%

Long-Term Effects

Many Americans got here to count on that the authorities would defend them from any monetary failures due to the New Deal's achievements. People relied on one another and themselves to continue to exist the Great Depression. They need to depend on the federal government as an opportunity, consistent with the New Deal.

To hold the rate of the dollar, FDR modified the gold standard. That set up a precedent, which led President Richard Nixon to absolutely abolish it in 1973.

Chapter 3: Implications Of The Great Depression

Who changed into laid low with the Great Depression?

The Great Depression had a electricity on almost all of us, despite the fact that not everyone changed into affected within the equal manner. Even individuals who did not lose their jobs due to the reduced degrees of funding and financial development no matter the truth that had some adverse results. For example, it might be more difficult to advantage a mortgage or a small employer mortgage if a close-by bank failed. The affects have been visible internationally as well, and numerous countries had similar economic reductions.

What have been the Great Depression's preliminary consequences?

The 1929 inventory marketplace disintegrate have emerge as a quick and catastrophic one. Banks started out to fall due to the economic community's response. This decreased corporation hobby not on time financial development and raised the unemployment price. It took longer to determine the entire effect of the Great Depression due to the ripple consequences. For example, the unemployment price didn't reap its high for four years.

The Great Depression and Women

Women have been the best American demographic to experience project boom for the duration of the Great Depression. The sort of operating ladies in the United States superior with the aid of using 24 percent amongst 1930 and 1940, from 10.Five million to 13 million. The Great Depression's financial strains forced ladies to are looking for employment in ever-increasing numbers as male breadwinners out of vicinity their jobs, but the reality that girls had been step by step becoming a member of the difficult paintings for many years. Between 1929 and 1939, the marriage charge fell through 22%, which brought on an increase in the kind of single women seeking out paintings. First Lady Eleanor Roosevelt, who pushed her husband for additonal ladies in office—including Secretary of Labor Frances Perkins, the primary woman to keep a cabinet position—have come to be a effective champion for women throughout the Great Depression. Nursing, coaching, and home artwork were most of the lower-paying however more robust jobs available to women sooner or later of the financial disaster. In FDR's speedy developing management, secretarial positions improved and took their place. However, there has been a seize: greater than 25% of National Recovery Administration wage regulations particular decrease charges for women, and occupations made underneath the WPA constrained women to professions like nursing and stitching that paid an lousy lot less than the ones assigned to men. Married ladies had to overcome more boundaries:

By 1940, marriage prohibitions had been imposed in 26 states due to the fact running better halves were seen to be displacing succesful-bodied men from their occupations, regardless of the fact that during truth they had been filling positions that guys would no longer choice and incomes plenty much less coins.

SOURCES OF RECOVERY

It isn't always surprising that foreign cash devaluations and financial expansion had been the precept drivers of recuperation spherical the sector given the crucial roles that monetary contraction and the gold sizeable done in producing the Great Depression. The durations even as global places deserted the gold preferred (or appreciably depreciated their currencies) coincided with intervals of manufacturing growth that had formerly slowed. For instance, while the united states did not considerably depreciate its forex till 1933, Britain, that have turn out to be pushed off the gold preferred in September 1931, recovered instead fast. Similar to this, Argentina and Brazil in Latin America, which started out to devalue in 1929, went via fantastically slight downturns and had usually recovered with the beneficial resource of 1935. In evaluation, the economic manufacturing inside the "Gold Bloc" international locations of Belgium and France, that have been especially devoted to the gold large and slow to devalue, end up however drastically decrease in 1935 than it had been in 1929.

Devaluation, but, had a hint direct effect on production. Instead, it general worldwide places to increase their coins deliver with out stressful approximately changes inside the rate of gold or the rate in their forex. Countries that benefited extra from this pliability had stronger healing. Early in 1933, the us saw especially robust economic increase. Between 1933 and 1937, the American cash deliver rose with the aid of approximately 42%. This economic growth changed into in most instances the give up give up end result of a big gold influx into the US, which have become in part sparked thru the escalating political unrest in Europe in advance than World War II. By bringing down hobby expenses and increasing credit score score options, monetary growth boosted consumption. Additionally, it extended expectancies of inflation in area of deflation, presenting capacity borrowers greater guarantee that, want to they decide to borrow cash, their profits and income might be ok to pay once more the mortgage. The reality that consumer and company expenditure on hobby-touchy objects like automobiles, motors, and machinery extended a long manner extra hastily than purchaser spending on services is one indication that economic boom spurred a healing within the United States through selling borrowing.

In order to sell healing in the US, economic policy emerge as first-class a minor component. In reality, the Revenue Act of 1932 notably raised tax charges within the United States if you need to balance the federal fee range, which had the accidental end result of in addition discouraging expenditure and inflicting the economic machine to mention no. Early in 1933, Franklin D. Roosevelt launched the New Deal, which did function a number of of recent federal duties purported to spur economic growth. For instance, the Tennessee Valley Authority (TVA) constructed dams and energy plant life in a in particular impoverished vicinity, at the equal time as the Works Progress Administration (WPA) recruited the jobless to artwork on authorities-constructing tasks. However, in comparison to the dimensions of the financial gadget, each the actual increases in authorities expenditure and the rate variety deficit were modest. When nation authorities charge variety deficits are taken underneath consideration, this will grow to be very smooth because of the reality those deficits surely decreased on the equal time as the federal deficit improved. As a result, the New Deal's new spending duties had little of an actual economic expansionary impact. However, it is unsure if they will have had a superb effect on purchaser and corporation mood. It's viable that some New Deal projects made recovery harder. For instance, the National Recovery Administration (NRA), which pushed groups in each employer to adopt a code of conduct, was set up below the National Industrial Recovery Act of 1933. These felony guidelines prohibited charge opposition among organizations, established industry-unique minimal salaries, or maybe constrained output. The Agricultural Adjustment Administration (AAA), which established voluntary guidelines and provided farmers with incentive bills to restrict output in the hopes of enhancing agricultural expenses, changed into mounted via the Agricultural Adjustment Act of 1933. The early levels of america' recuperation had been marked with the useful resource of inflation and a disincentive to reemployment and production, consistent with present day studies on such anticompetitive behaviors and pay and pricing standards.

A further separate recession that commenced in May 1937 and lasted until June 1938 lessen short the American healing. The Federal Reserve's preference to noticeably decorate reserve requirements was one of the reasons of the melancholy of 1937–1938. This movement, which modified into advocated with the useful resource of using concerns that there may be a speculative more inside the financial device, stopped the money supply from all at once growing and actually led it to say no another time. The slump is also believed to were inspired thru monetary contraction and a decline in inventory funding added on through difficult paintings strife. The vital motive why america stayed depressed for the entire decade is that the united states of a went via a second, very immoderate contraction in advance than it had truly recovered from the massive lack of the early Thirties.

Only a small a part of the revival of the American financial system changed into because of World War II. Real GDP within the United States changed into some distance above its pre-Depression stage with the resource of 1939 but the despair of 1937–1938, and with the useful resource of 1941 it had recovered to indoors round 10% of its lengthy-run trend path. Therefore, in advance than navy expenditure started out to visibly increase, america had essentially recovered to a amazing amount. The unemployment price in 1941 became simply under 10%, and the USA monetary device have grow to be moreover pretty off-style at the onset of the battle. Due to the army buildup, the government's finances deficit prolonged appreciably in 1941 and 1942. At the identical time, the Federal Reserve appreciably elevated the cash supply in reaction to the chance and later reality of warfare. In addition to big conscription that started out out in 1942, those expansionary economic and monetary regulations helped to unexpectedly placed the economic system lower back on direction and get the unemployment price all of the manner right down to its pre-Depression diploma. The struggle, therefore, had a issue in finishing the healing to finish employment, regardless of the truth that it became now not the number one motive force of the healing inside the United States. The contribution of increased government spending, especially at the army, to economic restoration, differed extensively among international locations. Similar to the united states, Great Britain did no longer installation economic expansion to a big diploma inside the early tiers of its restoration. However, it did extensively enhance military spending after 1937. In an try to shield the gold present day, France extended taxes in the middle of the 1930s, however beginning in 1936, it had massive finances deficits. However, a law that decreased the French workweek from forty six to 40 hours—a diploma that extended costs and reduced production—quite offset the expansionary effect of those deficits. Germany and Japan carried out a economic coverage with extra success. Early inside the restoration, the German fee variety deficit as a percentage of GDP climbed quality modestly; but, after 1934, because of expenditure on public works and rearmament, it appreciably elevated. Between 1932 and 1934, Japan's authorities spending, specially at the navy, multiplied from 31 to 38 percent of the usa's GDP, leading to big price range deficits. With the assist of this monetary stimulus, big monetary growth, and a depreciated yen, the Japanese monetary device rapid reached full employment.

Chapter 4: The End Of The Great Depression

Politically and economically, the 1930s had been a difficult decade for max of the arena. The 1929 inventory marketplace crash and the following economic depression inside the United States brought about big unemployment, which with the aid of manner of early 1933 had reached up to twenty-5% of the body of workers (extra than twelve million employees). Most different personnel had their earnings reduced. The early years of the Depression (1929–33) have been presided over with the resource of the use of President Herbert Hoover (1874–1964), who made most effective sporadic comments. Americans misplaced religion in Hoover due to the truth the financial machine deteriorated, and there has been a brilliant deal of social unrest. When he took place of business in early 1933 after being elected president in 1932, Franklin Roosevelt (1882–1945) inspired optimism collectively with his first rate New Deal social and economic rehabilitation obligations. Roosevelt took a hard stance, however the slump did now not dramatically get higher. Economic problem in Europe sparked the emergence of immoderate sports, drastically the Nazi Party in Germany and Adolf Hitler (1889–1945).

Japan, Italy, and Germany all started out out out military enlargement schemes that worried occupying one-of-a-type worldwide locations with force.

Only a long time after the cease of World War I, another worldwide war finally broke out in Europe in September 1939. (1914–18). The Allies, notably america, Britain, China, and the Soviet Union, would possibly fight the Axis international locations, Germany, Japan, and Italy, in this new worldwide war. The US entered World War II with the surprising Japanese assault on Pearl Harbor on December 7, 1941. In 1942 and 1943, the U.S.'s get right of access to into the struggle sparked a entire commercial enterprise mobilization pressure. (Industrial mobilization includes the creation of splendid quantities of army hardware, which incorporates warships, tanks, weapons, and ammunition.) Through the 1930s, Roosevelt and company businesses had sharp disagreements over New Deal programs, however for the conflict mobilization attempt, he desired their guide. As a quit end result, numerous Roosevelt's tips and initiatives—in conjunction with the law of agency— brought to address the affects of the Great Depression would be scrapped. Millions of recent jobs were created inside the company manner to huge navy contracts, and income there have been greater than the ones during the Great Depression. The Great Depression have become in the end over manner to the growth in employment and salaries. Optimism approximately the us of the financial system decrease returned with improved military spending for the improvement of warfare device.

The Price of War.

The American authorities end up prepared to spend some factor it essential to win World War II considering that preventing expenses coins. From plenty less than $9 billion in 1939 to more than $90 five billion in 1945, the federal budget accelerated. The navy attempt fee $290 billion in all. Half of the finances have been acquired from normal taxation, with the alternative budget coming from the sale of battle bonds and loans. A national tax structure in case you need to remaining into the twenty first century became created by using the use of the usage of the Revenue Act of 1942. From $ninety billion in 1939 to $212 billion in 1945, the gross countrywide product (the sum of all commodities and services generated by manner of the usage of a rustic's employees) increased dramatically. By 1945, an first-rate amount of struggle resources were artificial. Nearly 3 hundred,000 bombers, 86,000 tanks, sixty four,000 touchdown ships, 6,000 naval vessels, heaps and lots of guns, billions of rounds of ammunition, and loads of thousands of automobiles and jeeps had all been produced in American centers. The United States on my own generated greater battle elements than the combined output of the Axis international locations (Germany, Italy, and Japan).

Unwilling Nation

The prevent of World War I (1914–18) in Europe had brought peace, however no longer wealth. Germany had intense economic issues following the stop of the struggle, and people problems provided a platform for Adolf Hitler and the Nazi Party. Hitler vowed to reinforce Germany's army an outstanding way to repair its energy. The Japanese military, which had pastimes to conquer China and distinct East Asian countries, ousted a inclined civilian authorities in Japan on the equal time. Japan, which has few natural assets, needed to have manage over the ones positioned in its buddies. President Roosevelt inside the United States stored a cautious, traumatic eye at the growing worldwide typhoon. The American public, for the maximum detail, had no preference to get worried in some different war; World War I were sufficient. As a end end result, he had little manual as he organized for each other struggle. The "warfare to give up all wars" have come to be what it have become dubbed. In the period in-between, Hitler's German infantrymen started out sweeping over Europe. In September 1939, at the equal time as Germany invaded Poland, Britain and France declared conflict on Germany, thereby beginning World War II. Because the united states should need to bring together a massive army stress and bring hundreds of war gadget if it entered the struggle. Roosevelt recommended the us of a that it became crucial to start making arrangements for a ability battle even on the same time because the USA turn out to be nonetheless formally impartial. Roosevelt became worried that if Germany conquered Europe and Britain, the US may be the subsequent u . S . To cope with its brave and properly-prepared military.

Government And Industry At Odds

Roosevelt and the personal region had exceptional thoughts approximately a way to prepare the us of the united states for war. The U.S. Become required to shift privately held businesses from domestic to battle manufacturing, enhance mining and processing of raw substances applied in manufacture, adjust raw cloth distribution, and control military purchases of battle commodities that allows you to efficiently mobilize the u . S .. The biggest corporations within the u.S.A. Have lengthy served because the military's essential contractors. However, Roosevelt's New Dealers sought to put off this dependency on large industries with the useful resource of awarding contracts for the conflict to small companies as nicely. They have been especially interested by awarding navy contracts to smaller organizations situated in areas of the kingdom that have been even though feeling the impacts of the Great Depression. They believed that the mobilization method want to be consolidated in effective government companies that might arrange the general battle attempt to offer contracts to a sizeable variety of businesses sooner or later of the united states. On the opportunity difficulty, the bulk of industries did not need the government to meddle with their monetary markets or halt the manufacture of home devices. They concept the conflict can also save you quick and did not need to reveal it proper into a brief-term venture and forfeit the income they were presently making as the us started to slowly emerge from the Great Depression. They preferred that best facilities constructed with public cash or with special economic arrangements in authorities contracts that assured they may make tremendous earnings might be used to provide army items. Additionally, they preferred to live as loose as viable from the difficult paintings and social reforms of the New Deal. Businesses expected greater stringent guidelines at some point of times of conflict and the set up order of latest, extended-lasting federal businesses that could oversee military mobilization and in all likelihood even the positioned up-struggle US financial system. They urged that commercial enterprise corporation volunteering coordinated through transitory authorities corporations that is probably rapid destroyed after the warfare should be the idea for mobilization. In order to oversee industrial mobilization, Roosevelt had to rely on a number of small brief corporations which have been heavily staffed with non-public business corporation advisers, people of organization advisory committees, and navy personnel. However, the kingdom's corporation leaders antagonistic the appearance of any massive New Deal-like organizations. The War Resources Board (WRB) became initially mounted with the resource of Roosevelt in overdue 1939 to put together the dominion's organization. The WRB became the preliminary mobilization business enterprise in a line of them. It created a method centered on unforced commercial collaboration. However, due to the fact the enterprise become nevertheless hesitant to transform and the general public despite the fact that did now not truely assist mobilization, the plan to interchange industries from domestic to army production became in no manner really completed.

As fast as Germany conquered France in June 1940, the United States commenced out sending shipments of food and unique resources to Britain. After prevailing a second time period in office in November 1940, Roosevelt installation the Office of Production Management (OPM) in January 1941 to start the economic manufacturing of warfare substances. William Knudsen (1879–1948), a former GM chairman, served because the OPM's director. Similar to the WRB, the OPM had trouble persuading groups to replace from generating civilian products to producing military devices.

A new partnership between business enterprise employer and the authorities.

The United States got here into World War II a ways later than it did in the First World War. The United States' complete mobilization began out on December 7, 1941, while the Japanese attacked Pearl Harbor. More than 3 hundred airplanes launched a surprise assault at the U.S. Pacific Fleet if you want to save you the united states from opposing Japan's ongoing military buildup inside the Far East, substantially within the Philippines, wherein the usa had massive pastimes. The American populace changed into startled and incensed via manner of the lack of 3700 lives within the United States. The following day, December eight, america declared conflict on Japan. Germany and Italy each declared conflict on the United States 3 days later.

The War Production Board (WPB) modified into primarily based by using the use of way of President Roosevelt within the next month, January 1942, to take duty for wartime mobilization. The human beings now supported government efforts to mobilize business enterprise significantly extra fiercely due to the urgency of the proclaimed war. Industries have been now forced to switch to generating for the military. The WPB attempted to allocate employees and uncooked belongings to the sectors that have been maximum crucial for development. To ensure that uncooked property like metal and aluminum is probably used to create weapons, the manufacturing of severa own family devices, like toasters, automobiles, and refrigerators, became significantly curtailed or stopped altogether. The business region commenced out operating on a 24-hour shift basis.

Roosevelt moreover gave financial and crook incentives to companies to comply with the mobilization requirements further to delaying the approval of every other New Deal measures intended to manipulate the organisation, including hard work prison tips restricting salaries and maximum hours labored. Roosevelt had the minimal prison authority to simply positioned into impact conversion, notwithstanding the reality that the enterprise become "compelled" to mobilize. In order to lessen conflicts with industry leaders, incentives have been deployed. These incentives blanketed huge tax discounts for constructing new centers to fabricate conflict objects, the suspension of unique tips to allow rival agencies to art work collectively as an alternative, and the issuance of navy conflict manufacturing contracts with earnings ensures. To guarantee more green employer collaboration, Roosevelt essentially handed the kingdom's agency leaders manipulate of the wartime monetary gadget.

Roosevelt decided on Republican Henry L. Stimson (1867–1951) as secretary of battle that allows you to hold the usa of the united states collectively on the equal time as acknowledging the position that industrial corporation had in figuring out American mobilization coverage. Stimson, a fervent supporter of big commercial organization, took the initiative in coordinating battle preparations with business enterprise titans.

Manufacturing contracts were especially given to the maximum vital groups below Stimson's path because of the truth that they'd massive workforces, installed assembly lines, and studies divisions.

Government commercial enterprise advisors argued that those big corporations may also need to most with out problems switch from civilian to navy manufacturing. As a cease end result, one-zero.33 of all military contracts went to the pinnacle 10 companies, leaving smaller businesses to at the complete compete for smaller contracts with the number one groups. The amount of ships, tanks, aircraft, guns, and ammunition created within the period that accompanied turned into terrific. Government and employer responsibilities have all at once shifted. In order to stabilize the unstable financial machine sooner or later of the Great Depression, the federal government assumed the initiative with robust well-known backing. However, the agency is not partial to some of the policies that came with authorities monetary manual. The warfare positioned businesses in a strong negotiating function because the U.S. Authorities had an urgent need for enterprise production. With little assist from the government, they had been able to set their non-public terms, cast off New Deal boundaries, and interest on greater income.

Mobilization advances.

As extra than 5 million Americans enlisted inside the struggle, difficult paintings shortages without delay superior, in stark evaluation to the 1930s' excessive unemployment charge. The economic device started out luring in new employees, along with ladies and those of shade. There has been an growth in opposition in some unspecified time in the future of industries for the exertions pool. The War Manpower Commission (WMC) have grow to be set up in April 1942 to help with hard work shortages. This corporation assigned employees to the most critical occupations. In order to in addition relieve the hard paintings crisis, President Roosevelt loosened some of the difficult paintings tips mounted location by the usage of the New Deal in 1938 in February 1943. He mandated a minimal 40-eight-hour workweek for personnel in a few key businesses and specially regions of america wherein there was a labor scarcity. The WMC determined the sectors and regions a very good way to be impacted. Particularly in sectors that produced steel, electric powered device, ships, airplanes, cars, and one in all a kind transportation-related gadgets, the ones reforms notably improved employees' wages. In 1943, disagreements among industries over access to labor and uncooked substances in addition to special manufacturing-related issues endured as mobilization moved forward. In order to settle the disagreements, Roosevelt installation the Office of War Mobilization (OWM), a tiny transient commercial enterprise organisation, in May 1943. The OWM, led with the resource of former Justice James F. Byrnes (1879–1972) of the U.S. Supreme Court, assisted in coordinating efforts among severa corporations.

The transition to a wartime financial device became frequently finished by means of July 1943. A massive Allied pressure may land inside the French place of Normandy less than a 12 months later. A great turning component inside the struggle became marked by using using the Allied troops' seeming victory inside the course of the German forces at some point of this a success invasion to retake Western Europe. Even despite the reality that there were despite the fact that severa months of immoderate struggle, Germany would ultimately fall. In May 1945, Germany formally surrendered, bringing an stop to the European War. After the united states detonated atomic bombs on Hiroshima and Nagasaki in September 1945, Japan agreed to a right peace treaty.

EFFECTS OF MOBILIZATION

The U.S. Financial system became significantly boosted with the useful resource of warfare mobilization after extra than 10 years of economic stagnation. During the struggle, the United States pace of manufacturing of services and products extra than quadrupled, and employment in the long run reached 98 percentage of the workforce. In 1939, there were nine million unemployed human beings in a country that emerge as although seeking out to get over the Great Depression. Just six years later, in 1945, that variety fell to a million. Private organisation and business corporation had delivered many new personnel, and the federal government had expanded significantly all through the warfare. The variety of federal civilian employees extended through four hundred percent among 1941 and 1945, persevering with a fashion that commenced out all through the Great Depression. In the enterprise organization and public sectors mixed, seventeen million new jobs were generated.

More human beings have been incomes earnings than in advance than because of the abundance of latest occupations that have been turning into available. Throughout the years of the battle, their hourly wages rose with the useful useful resource of twenty-two%. By the center of 1943, more than eight million production employees, or almost 60% of all earnings earners, made among 50 cents and $1 ordinary with hour, with 3% of people incomes greater than $1.50. These fees had been a ways higher than what that that they had at some level in the Great Depression. Debts collected inside the direction of the Great Depression have been settled, and reserves commenced to increase. Corporate executives reclaimed their misplaced political effect and status thru the mobilization of struggle. After being abandoned after 1929, commercial enterprise towns had been alternatively profitable with the aid of 1943.

Farms moreover made a recovery. As meals name for prolonged to gasoline the Allied infantrymen and agricultural output in Europe have become critically hampered all through the struggle, crop expenses extra than doubled. Profits for farmers rose. Farmers all another time benefited from prosperity following twenty years of economic issues. From 1939 to 1944, farm income multiplied from $five.Three billion to $thirteen.6 billion. Farm cities flourished, and a number of them rose to prominence economically.

The Great Depression changed into in part alleviated with the useful resource of the New Deal regulations installed vicinity after 1933, however it needed a big army buildup to area an give up to it. The New Dealers generally vanished into the facts due to the fact the financial machine of the u . S . Grew more potent.

The New Deal Programs End

Roosevelt's advertising advertising and marketing marketing campaign for social and economic transformation had inside the maximum crucial ended through the usage of 1940. Up until Roosevelt revised his domestic coverage, a conservative Congress and numerous business company executives who firmly idea that New Deal responsibilities improperly encroached on private enterprise had accrued enough political clout to halt conflict mobilization. Roosevelt had to lessen the federal authorities's dedication to social transformation on the way to get america of the united states prepared for war. Many dedicated fanatics of the regime started defecating in unhappiness. Numerous New Deal applications have been near down at some point of the subsequent few years. Other wonderful New Deal tasks got here to a halt throughout World War II, despite the truth that Social Security, the Securities and Exchange Commission, agriculture programs, and one-of-a-type projects ought to maintain after the warfare. For instance, the Civilian Conservation Corps (CCC), one of the extra famous New Deal duties and a particular favored of Roosevelt's, became discontinued in 1942. The CCC end up initially based totally in 1933 to rent more youthful guys for jobs enhancing public lands. The CCC commenced teaching people in reading blueprints and special duties that is probably useful inside the army as quickly as World War II started out out out. Roosevelt advertised the CCC as a useful business enterprise for children under the army age as increasingly CCC humans were enlisting in the military. Congress, but, decreased financing because of the truth they idea the CCC became in too much opposition with the personal area. The battle employer, which provided extra pay and employment possibilities, furthermore fee the Works Progress Administration (WPA), any other New Deal initiative, the majority of its body of employees. The WPA, founded in 1935, became abolished at the stop of 1943. The National Youth Administration (NYA), which end up hooked up in 1935 as well, persevered to characteristic until 1943, in massive component due to its success in instructing younger humans in trades that would be vital inside the battle industries.

End of the New Deal

By 1943, business mobilization have become whole, and Roosevelt began out thinking about the postwar American financial device. The National Resources Planning Board (NRPB), a 1933 New Deal agency, turn out to be tasked through the president with developing a postwar method. The NRPB became first set up to supervise employer recovery at a few degree within the Depression's early years. The board anticipated that the warfare industries ought to hire fewer humans even as returning to generating home items at the same time as getting ready for the usa of a's postwar financial machine.

Chapter 5: What Was The Great Depression?

We all comprehend about the Great Depression. Many humans dread a 2nd one, and particularly because it turned into one of the fundamental sports activities that inaugurated World War 2, with a number of different causes that contributed to it.

The Great Depression changed right into a large time period round the arena monetary melancholy that started out within the U.S.A. Inside the Nineteen Thirties and lasted until 1945. The Great Depression started out in 1929 in maximum countries and lasted until the overdue Thirties in others. It grow to be the 20th century's longest, inmost, and most commonplace despair. The Great Depression is often used for example of the intensity with which the worldwide financial tool can degrade.

Do you need to recognize why the Great Depression occurred, what outcomes it had on people, and the manner the world recovered from it? Then hold going and study or pay attention to this e-book.

The Great Depression started out inside the U.S.A. After a wonderful drop in stock values that started out round September 4th, 1929 and culminated inside the stock exchange crash of October twenty-ninth, 1929, that made worldwide headings (known as Black Tuesday). Between 1929 and 1932, the global GDP reduced with the aid of way of almost 15%. In instance, at a few degree within the Great Economic catastrophe, global GDP decreased with the useful resource of using much less than 1% from 2008 to 2009. By the mid-Thirties, some economies had started out to get better. Having said that, the effects of the Great Depression remained in many nations till the outbreak of the second international conflict.

Both upscale and terrible worldwide places had been devastated through using the Great Depression. Personal profits, tax income, income, and charges all reduced, on the identical time as worldwide change reduced through over half. Joblessness inside the U.S. Has extended to 23%, with charges as immoderate as 33% in unique global places. Cities all all through the world have been substantially harmed, in particular those reliant on heavy marketplace. In many countries, constructing and advent has come to a prevent. Crop charges plunged by using manner of the use of virtually 60%, unfavorable farming cities and backwoods. Parts relying upon essential location companies like mining and logging suffered the most because of falling want and a lack of possibility property of work.

The rapid and dreadful disintegrate of United States inventory exchange prices, which started out on October twenty-fourth, 1929, is usually seen because the stimulate of the Great Depression via the usage of financial historians. Even so, some say that the stock trade crash end up a sign of the Great Depression in vicinity of a reason.

Even after the 1929 Wall Street Crash, while the Dow Jones Industrial Average fell from 381 to 198 in 2 months, there has been a duration of optimism. The stock change commenced out to rise in early 1930, with the Dow Jones Industrial Average recuperating to 294 (pre-melancholy levels) inside the month of April 1930, in advance than falling slowly for severa years, wearing out a low of 41 in 1932.

Federal governments and companies in the beginning spent greater within the first half of of 1930 than in the former twelve months's comparable duration. Customers, rather, who had suffered terrific losses within the inventory exchange the preceding year, decreased their spending via 10%. A devastating dry spell stricken the farming heartland of the U.S. Beginning inside the mid-Thirties.

By the mid-Thirties, rates of hobby had dropped to historically low stages, however predicted deflation and people's endured hostility to acquiring supposed that customer spending and economic funding stayed low.

Auto earnings had fallen right beneath the ones of 1928 with the aid of manner of May 1930. Costs started to fall in well-known, though profits stayed consistent in 1930. In 1931, a deflationary spiral started out. Farmers' monetary potential clients had been intensified via way of falling crop charges and a dry spell in the Great Plains. In spite of federal assist, almost 10% of all Great Plains farms changed arms in some unspecified time in the future of the Great Depression.

In the start, the fall within the U.S. Financial tool grow to be the pressure that dragged down most specific international locations; in a while, each u . S .'s intrinsic defects or strengths worsened or reduced the situation.

Individual nations' frenzied efforts to aid their economies thru protectionist regulations-- similar to the United States' Smoot-- Hawley Tariff Act of 1930 and vindictive rate lists in exquisite nations-- magnified the global alternate fall apart, resulting inside the melancholy. By 1933, the financial recession had decreased global trade to at least one-1/three of what it were 4 years before.

Chapter 6: What Triggered The Great Depression?

Throughout the Crash of 1929 preceding the Great Depression, margin necessities have been fine 10%. Brokerage companies, to place it absolutely, would possibly mortgage $nine for each single $1 a financier had transferred. When the market fell, retailers employed the ones loans, which could not be repaid. Banks commenced to flop as borrowers defaulted on coins debt and depositors attempted to withdraw their deposits en masse, activating severa monetary group runs. Federal authorities assurances and Federal Reserve banking tips to save you such panics were inefficient or now not used. Bank disasters introduced on the loss of billions of dollars in belongings.

Arrearages ended up being heaps heavier, really due to the fact fees and profits fell by way of using 20-- 50% but the economic duties stayed at the exact same greenback quantity. After the panic of 1929 and within the path of the first ten months of 1930, 744 USA banks failed. (In all, nine,000 banks failed at some diploma in the Thirties.) By April 1933, round $7 billion in deposits had been frozen in failed banks or the ones left unlicensed after the March Bank Vacation. Bank failures grew out of control as decided creditors hired loans that borrowers did now not have time or coins to pay lower again. With destiny profits searching horrible, capital rate and building slowed or clearly stopped. In the face of horrific loans and getting worse destiny potential clients, the making it through banks ended up being an awful lot more conservative of their financing. Banks superior their capital reserves and made lots less loans, which magnified deflationary pressures. A vicious circle superior and the down spiral accelerated.

The liquidation of economic debt could not maintain up with the autumn of prices that it brought about. The mass have an effect on of the stampede to liquidate prolonged the fee of every dollar owed, relative to the price of decreasing possession holdings. The very attempt of humans to decrease their burden of monetary debt effectively accelerated it. Paradoxically, the greater the debtors paid, the greater they owed. This self-stressful method grew to become a 1930 monetary catastrophe proper right into a 1933 first rate despair.

Fisher's debt-deflation concept on the begin did no longer have traditional impact due to the counter-argument that debt-deflation represented no greater than a redistribution from one enterprise (debtors) to any other (lenders). Pure re-distributions need to don't have any big macroeconomic affects.

Building on both the financial speculation of Milton Friedman and Anna Schwartz and the monetary debt deflation hypothesis of Irving Fisher, Ben Bernanke advanced an opportunity approach which the financial predicament impacted output. He builds on

Fisher's argument that large decreases within the value degree and small income result in increasing actual cash debt troubles, which in turn reasons debtor insolvency and as a end result decreases mixture want; every other rate degree lower should then motive a economic responsibility deflationary spiral. According to Bernanke, a hint decrease inside the price degree sincerely reallocates wealth from borrowers to financial institutions without doing damage to the economic machine. However, while the deflation is excessive, falling assets expenses in addition to debtor insolvencies result in a decrease within the small rate of property on bank stability sheets. Banks will reply via the usage of tightening their credit score situations, which in turn results in a credit crunch that substantially hurts the monetary gadget. A credit score score crunch decreases financial funding and intake, which results in lowering aggregate want and moreover provides to the deflationary spiral.

Because of the counter-argument that debt-deflation become simply nothing greater than a redistribution from one organization (debtors) to every other, Fisher's debt-deflation concept within the beginning did not have favored approval (economic institutions). Re-distributions for the purpose of re-distribution want to don't have any macroeconomic repercussions.

Ben Bernanke designed an possibility way of taking a have a look at how the economic seize 22 situation impacted output, based totally upon each Milton Friedman and Anna Schwartz's economic hypothesis and Irving Fisher's debt deflation hypothesis. He counts on Fisher's idea that sharp drops inside the fee diploma and small income bring about growing actual cash debt issues, which reasons debtor insolvency and reduces aggregate need; a further drop inside the fee diploma can also then cause a financial duty deflationary spiral. Bernanke claims that a small drop within the fee level in reality reallocates cash from borrowers to lenders without triggering economic damage. When deflation is extreme, no matter the truth that, decreasing belongings fees blended with debtor private bankruptcies cause the small price of assets on financial agency balance sheets to plunge. Banks will react thru tightening up credit score situations, main to a credit score crunch with a purpose to significantly damage the monetary device. A credit score rating score restrict decreases economic funding and intake, vital to weaker aggregate need and rushing up the deflationary cycle.

The Hypothesis of Expectations

Expectations have become a key a part of macroeconomic models due to the truth the economic mainstream embraced the brand new neoclassical synthesis. A tremendous handling of public expectancies, in line with Peter Temin, Barry Wigmore, Gauti B. Eggertsson, and Christina Romer, turn out to be the vital element to restoration and finishing the Great Depression. The idea is based totally upon the truth that in the month of March 1933, whilst Franklin D. Roosevelt took place of work, terrific monetary indices turned super after years of deflation and an immoderate financial downturn. Customer charges commenced to rise after a period of deflation, industrial production peaked inside the month of March 1933, and financial funding greater than doubled in 1933, following a flip-round within the month of March 1933. There have been no economic pressures at paintings to make clear the alternate. The coins supply went right now to lower, while quick-variety charges of interest stayed spherical zero. Many human beings expected greater deflation and an monetary downturn in advance than March 1933, so even rates of interest at 0 did now not stimulate financial investment. Most humans started out to assume inflation and economic boom while Roosevelt introduced massive ordinary modifications. Rates of hobby at 0 began to sell financial funding as forecasted due to these top notch expectancies. Roosevelt's shift in economic and financial coverage made his policy targets extra practicable. Need and economic investment were stimulated via manner of the use of the expectancy of superior destiny earnings and better destiny inflation. The desertion of coverage dogmas just like the gold requirement, a nicely-balanced spending plan in instances of crisis, and minimal federal government, in keeping with the studies, precipitated an endogenous considerable shift in expectancy that represented about 70-- 80% of the rebound in output and expenses from 1933 to 1937. If this system shift had now not passed off and Hoover's rules had preserved, the financial device might also want to have persevered its quick collapse in 1933, with output being 30% decrease in 1937 than it grow to be in 1933.

Fears the various population that the slight tightening up of monetary and monetary coverage in 1937 became the initial step within the direction of convey back the pre-1933 coverage routine caused the financial downturn of 1937-- 38, which avoided economic healing from the Great Depression.

Financial experts these days concur that the federal authorities and reserve financial institution should engage to preserve the interrelated macroeconomic aggregates of gdp and coins deliver on a robust improvement path. To keep away from a fall apart in cash supply and aggregate want, reserve banks need to enhance liquidity inside the banking machine, and the federal authorities must cut taxes and accelerate charge if a recession is predicted.

Most financial professionals trusted Say's law and the market's equilibrating powers at the start of the Great Depression, and for this reason misjudged the depth of the disaster. The Austrian School financial specialists were consentaneous of their assist for at once-out leave-it-by myself liquidationism. According to the liquidationist mind-set, an tension works to liquidate unsuccessful corporation and monetary investments which have been rendered old via clinical development, maximizing elements of production (capital and labor) to be redeployed in more green elements of the colourful economic system. They said that self-adjustment of the economic gadget changed into however the quality technique, even though it brought on big private bankruptcies.

President Herbert Hoover strove to preserve the federal fee variety plan stabilized until 1932, at the same time as he lost depend on his Secretary of the Treasury Andrew Mellon and changed him, consistent with economic experts like Barry Eichengreen and J. Bradford DeLong.

Many monetary historiographers maintain in mind that many Federal Reserve policymakers' strength of mind to the liquidationist attitude caused ravaging results. At the time of the early years of the Great Depression, a chief quantity of the capital stock wasn't redeployed however disappeared, contrary to the expectancies of liquidationists. The financial downturn added about net capital assemble-as an awful lot as be as an awful lot as pre-1924 ranges through way of the usage of 1933, in line with a studies have a examine thru Olivier Blanchard and Lawrence Summers. Leave-it-on my own liquidationism, in line with Milton Friedman, is "devastating absurdity."

Chapter 7: Nonconformist Ideas About The Depression

Austrian financial professional Friedrich Hayek and American monetary professional Murray Rothbard, who wrote America's Great Depression, are 2 vital thinkers inside the Austrian School on the Great Depression (1963). Like the monetarists, they take delivery of as actual with the Federal Reserve (advanced in 1913) bears a quite big percentage of the blame; however, in region of the Monetarists, they keep in mind the essential purpose for the Depression changed into the upward push of the cash supply inside the Nineteen Twenties, which ended in an unsustainable credit-fueled boom.

According to Austrian concept, cash deliver inflation delivered on an unsustainable increase in ownership values (shares and bonds) and additionally capital merchandise. Consequently, by the point the Federal Reserve tightened up in 1928, it turned into an extended manner too beyond because of preserve from an economic downturn. Hayek launched a paper in the month of February 1929 caution that the Federal Reserve's policies might result in a catch 22 situation within the inventory and credit score markets.

According to Rothbard, federal authorities assist for failing companies and attempts to preserve profits above market levels truely brought to the Depression's prolongation.

Unlike Rothbard, Hayek felt that the Federal Reserve had worsened the Depression's issues through permitting the cash deliver to agreement at the time of the early years of the Depression. Throughout the Depression, even though, Hayek chastised each the Federal Reserve and the Bank of England for not taking a extra contractionary function (in 1932 and 1934.

Hans Sennholz said that many the American financial system's booms and busts have been delivered about via the federal government generating a boom via easy coins and credit, which have become all at once discovered with the aid of way of the inescapable depression. After 5 years of unrestrained credit score rating growth with the beneficial useful resource of the Federal Reserve System underneath the Coolidge Administration, the amazing crash of 1929 happened. The catch 22 situation changed into worsened and lengthened via the passage of the Sixteenth Modification, the Federal Reserve Act, installing federal authorities deficits, the Hawley-Smoot Tariff Act, and the Income Act of 1932.

In the Nineteen Thirties, Ludwig von Mises wrote: "The deliver of actual gadgets can't be stepped forward with the useful resource of broadening credit. It amazing triggers a reorganization. It courses capital price from the route decided by using the use of the repute of the financial system and market situations. It triggers generating to study courses that it won't move until the monetary device have been given to more material merchandise. Subsequently, the increase is lacking a agency form. That isn't always genuine fulfillment. It's a fictitious fulfillment. It did no longer stand up from a benefit in economic wealth, i.E., the construct-up of fee savings that is probably positioned to inexperienced use. Rather, it came about because of the credit score score rating improvement, which gave the appearance of a lift. Ultimately, it will end up being easy that this monetary situation is based upon sand."

Waddill Catchings and William Trufant Foster, 2 economic experts from the Nineteen Twenties, promoted a hypothesis that impacted sure policymakers, which incorporates Herbert Hoover, Henry A. Wallace, Paul Douglas, and Marriner Eccles. It stated that the economic system produced greater than it took in sincerely due to the fact customers did no longer have enough profits. Subsequently, the Great Depression turn out to be introduced on through the unequal flow into of wealth at a few level within the Nineteen Twenties.

The main reason for the Great Depression, constant with this mind-set, have become a international over-funding in heavy marketplace capability contrasted with salaries and earning from independent businesses, like farms. The federal authorities turn out to be suggested as a treatment, with coins being pumped into the wallet of clients. That is, it want to re-inflate prices and profits to push as a bargain of the inflationary enhance in obtaining electricity into purchaser spending as possible at the same time as keeping the financial base. New factories were now not wanted due to the fact the financial device have been overbuilt. Foster and Catchings promoted that the federal and nation federal governments begin huge constructing responsibilities, a insurance that Hoover and Roosevelt accompanied.

It cannot be overemphasized that the general overall performance, output, and art work styles we are speaking about are lengthy-lasting and have been valid in advance than 1929. Those styles aren't the object of the triumphing financial downturn, nor are they the give up stop result of the second one worldwide warfare. The present day melancholy, as an opportunity, is the prevent end result of those lengthy-lasting propensities collapsing.

With electrification, mass manufacturing, and motorized farm gadget, monetary output skyrocketed in the first three a long time of the twentieth century, and due to the quick boom in overall performance, there was lots of extra production functionality and the artwork week have become being reduced. Spurgeon Bell is going over the big upward push in performance of big markets in the United

States, and the ramifications of overall performance on manufacturing, salaries, and the workweek, in his ebook Efficiency, Incomes, and National Salary (1940).

Chapter 8: The Cause And Effect Of The Depression

The critical transference system of the Great Depression changed into the gold requirement. Even worldwide locations that had in no way ever professional financial organization failures or monetary contraction were driven to embrace the deflationary technique because of the truth better expenses of hobby in deflationary global locations delivered approximately a gold outflow from international locations with lower prices of hobby. Nations who out of place gold however however desired to hold the gold requirement needed to allow their coins deliver and home fee degree to fall below the fee-- specie go with the flow system of the gold requirement (deflation).

There is popular association that protectionist policies much like the Smoot--Hawley Tariff Act added to the despair's getting worse.

According to a few economic studies, suspending gold convertibility (or deteriorating the foreign exchange in gold phrases) did the maximum to assist in healing, simply due to the truth the decline end up unfold out internationally with the useful resource of the gold requirement's rigidness.

At the time of the Great Depression, every brilliant distant places cash deserted the gold requirement. The U.K. Was the primary united states to accomplish that. Confronted with speculative assaults at the pound and diminishing gold reserves, the Bank of England stopped changing pound notes for gold inside the month of September 1931, and the pound became drifted on foreign exchange markets.

In 1931, Japan and the Scandinavian worldwide places signed up with the UK in deserting the gold requirement. Other countries, like Italy and america, stayed on the gold requirement till 1932 or 1933, whilst a little business agency of countries referred to as the "gold bloc," led with the beneficial useful resource of France and protected Poland, Belgium, and Switzerland, did so until 1935-- 36.

Later studies positioned that the rate with which a country left the gold basic precisely predicted its monetary restoration. The U.K. And Scandinavia, as an instance, who departed the gold requirement in 1931, recuperated an prolonged manner faster than France and Belgium, which remained on gold for loads longer. Nations with a silver requirement, like China, basically honestly stayed far from the Great Depression. Leaving the gold requirement has been validated to be a robust predictor of the seriousness of a rustic's melancholy and the term it calls for to recover for hundreds of nations, and that consists of developing ones. That allows to make easy why the depth and length of the melancholy differed a lot among elements and states everywhere.

International Trade Disturbance

Many financial specialists accept as true with that the massive drop in global change after 1930 worsened the depression, particularly for international locations which have been significantly depending on remote places trade. Two-thirds of American economic chroniclers felt that the Smoot-- Hawley Tariff Act (enacted June 17th, 1930) angry the Great Depression in a 1995 survey. Most historiographers and economic professionals blame this Act for worsening the Great Depression with the useful resource of manner of badly proscribing remote places change and activating vindictive rate lists in distinct international locations. While distant places change represented a small part of favored economic interest in the U.S. And was centered in a few markets like farming, it performed a drastically larger function in masses of various countries. In amongst 1921 and 1925, the standard industrial valorem charge of charge lists on dutiable imports have become 25.Nine%, but between 1931 and 1935, it skyrocketed to 50% beneath the new tariff. In monetary phrases, American exports decreased from almost $five.2 billion in 1929 to $1.7 billion in 1933 over the following 4 years; for that reason, no longer only did the real amount of exports disintegrate, but so did the charges. Wheat, cotton, tobacco, and lumber had been amongst the most hit farming items.

Federal governments all of the international over have taken masses of methods to lower their spending on imported merchandise, together with but no longer constrained to "imposing price lists, import constraints, and trade controls." These constraints introduced on an entire lot of anxiety amongst nations with a whole lot of bilateral trade, principal to high-quality export-import reduces in the course of the decline. Protectionism wasn't imposed gently with the resource of all administrations. Some international locations substantially elevated price lists and enforced severe constraints on foreign exchange operations, at the same time as others definitely in part reduced "alternate and change barriers":

Nations that stored their currencies ordinary and stayed at the gold requirement had been extra inclined to restriction overseas trade." "To enhance the stableness of bills and prevent gold losses," the ones global locations "grew to become to protectionist policies." They expected that through implementing the ones regulations and deficiencies, the financial decline can be stopped. Nations that dropped the gold requirement enabled their currencies to decrease, critical to a conditioning in their balance of payments. It moreover authorised reserve banks to loosen up economic coverage, allowing them to reduce fees of interest and characteristic as mortgage groups of very last choice. They did not really need protectionism virtually due to the fact that they'd the pleasant policy weapons to stand the Depression. " The duration and seriousness of a rustic's monetary despair, and the timing and electricity with which it recuperates, are all linked to truly how lengthy it come to be on the gold requirement. Early desertion of the gold requirement brought about small monetary downturns and fast healings in international locations that did so. Nations that stayed at the gold requirement, alternatively, treated prolonged durations of stagnancy."

The intro of the Smoot-Hawley Tariff worsened the Great Depression, steady with monetary specialists and financial historical analysts (in conjunction with Keynesians, Monetarists, and Austrian financial specialists), even though there can be struggle about how an lousy lot. According to conventional notion, the Smoot-Hawley Tariff became a prime contributor to the Great Depression. The Smoot-- Hawley Tariff Act, in line with the U.S. Senate internet web page on-line, is definitely one of the maximum devastating strategies in American records.

The British Banking Crisis of 1931 and the German Banking Crisis of 1931

In mid-1931, the economic dilemma spiraled out of control, starting with the failure of the Credit Anstalt in Vienna in May.

This placed quite a few pressure on Germany, which became already in a number of problem politically. With the escalation of Nazi and communist violence, and additionally financier jitters over the federal authorities's tough financial suggestions. As self-self belief plunged, financiers withdrew their short-variety charge variety from Germany. In the number one week of June, the Reichsbank out of place a hundred and fifty million marks, 540 million within the 2nd, and one hundred fifty million in 2 days, June 19-- 20. The prevent became on the horizon. President Herbert Hoover of the united states required a restriction on warfare reparations bills. That infuriated Paris, which depend on recurring German payments, but it snug the catastrophe, and a moratorium come to be consented to in the month of July 1931. Later in July, a global top in London produced no preparations, however on August 19th, Germany's overseas liabilities have been frozen for six months underneath a standstill affiliation. Personal banks in New York, and the Bank of International Settlements and the Bank of England, furnished emergency state of affairs financing to Germany. The cash actually slowed subjects down. In Germany, industrial disasters began out out, a prime financial organization closed in July, and all German banks had been given a two-day holiday. In July, commercial enterprise insolvencies ended up being greater trendy, infecting Romania and Hungary. The circumstance in Germany have been given worse, most important to political chaos that culminated in Hitler's Nazi application taking power within the month of January 1933.

The worldwide monetary capture 22 situation had now swallowed up Britain, and financiers from everywhere inside the international began taking flight £ 2.Five million nicely clearly well worth of gold from London each day.

The British capture 22 state of affairs modified into slowed, however not reversed, with the beneficial resource of £ twenty-five million credit score from the Bank of France and the Federal Reserve Bank of NY, and moreover a £ fifteen million fiduciary word problem.

In August 1931, the financial catch 22 situation activated a great political trap 22 state of affairs in the U.K. The lenders desired a well-balanced spending plan as deficits grew; Prime Minister Ramsay MacDonald's Labour manipulate concurred, offering to raise taxes, lessen spending, and, maximum controversially, decrease welfare thru manner of 20%. The Labour Party couldn't go through the attack on properly-being. MacDonald intended to retire, however King George V required that he live and installation a "National Federal government" of all occasions. The Conservative and Liberal events, and additionally a bit organisation of Labour leaders, signed on, while the large bulk of Labour leaders assaulted MacDonald for predominant the contemporary control as a traitor. Britain left the gold requirement and fared better than the the relaxation of the area at a few degree inside the Great Depression.

Chapter 9: How It Impacted Different Nations

Every nation inside the worldwide had been given hit via the global melancholy. However, a few international places had extra problems than others. Let's pick out severa for this financial disaster which may be superb.

The World Depression broke at a time even as the U.K. Had still not truly recuperated from the influences of the First World War greater than a whole decade earlier. The kingdom emerge as repelled the gold requirement in 1931.

The international financial capture 22 scenario started out out to weigh down Britain in 1931; financiers across the world started retreating their gold from London on the fee of £ 2.Five million each day. Credits of £ twenty-five million each from the Bank of France and the Federal Reserve Bank of NY and a issue of £ fifteen million fiduciary phrase slowed, however did no longer reverse the British catastrophe. The monetary seize 22 state of affairs now brought on a pinnacle political dilemma in Britain in the month of August 1931. With deficits installing, the lenders required a nicely balanced spending plan; the separated cupboard of Prime Minister Ramsay MacDonald's Labour federal government concurred; it proposed to raise taxes, cut spending and maximum controversially, to reduce welfare through the usage of 20%. The attack on well-being emerge as truely inappropriate to the Labour motion. MacDonald desired to give up, however King George V insisted he stay and shape an all-birthday party union "National Federal government". The Conservative and Liberals occasions signed on, collectively with a hint cadre of Labour, but the large bulk of Labour leaders knocked MacDonald as a traitor for fundamental the modern federal government. Britain went off the gold requirement and suffered reasonably a great deal less than one-of-a-kind huge global places in the Great Depression. In the 1931 British election, the Labour Party modified into nearly ruined, leaving MacDonald as Prime Minister for a particularly Conservative union.

The affects at the northern enterprise zones of Britain have been immediately and horrible, as need for trendy commercial objects collapsed. By the cease of 1930 joblessness had greater than doubled from 1 million to 2.5 million (20% of the insured hard work strain), and exports had fallen in price through manner of fifty%. In 1933, 30% of Glaswegians were out of labor because of the intense decrease in heavy marketplace. In some cities and cities within the north east, joblessness reached as excessive as 70% as shipbuilding fell with the useful resource of 90%. The National Appetite March of September-- October 1932 changed into the biggest of a series of cravings marches in Britain inside the Nineteen Twenties and Thirties. About 2 hundred,000 jobless men had been despatched out to the artwork camps, which persevered in operation till 1939.

In the an entire lot lots much less employer Midlands and Southern England, the effects were temporary and the later Thirties were a thriving time. Development in modern-day manufacture of electrical merchandise and a increase in the motor automobile marketplace modified into helped through a growing southern population and a broadening middle beauty. Farming furthermore noticed a boom eventually of this period.

The United States

Hoover's earliest anti-despair efforts relied on agencies' voluntary rejection to restriction their labor stress or cut earning, but corporations had no choice: earnings have been slashed, people had been laid off, and economic investments had been not on time.

The Smoot-- Hawley Tariff Act, surpassed within the month of June 1930, enforced responsibilities on severa imported devices. The Act's aim changed into to inspire human beings to shop for American-made objects with the resource of increasing the price of imported products, at the equal time as moreover generating sales for the federal authorities and protective farmers. In retaliation, maximum global places that traded with the us raised obligations on American-made devices, decreasing global change and intensifying the Depression.

Hoover requested creditors to form the National Credit Corporation in 1931 in order that big banks may also help struggling businesses in enduring. Bankers, however, had been reluctant to put money into failing corporations, and the National Credit Corporation did little to remedy the difficulty.

Joblessness had reached 23.6 percentage by way of the usage of 1932, peaking at twenty-5 percent in early 1933.

Dry spell persevered within the farming heartland, organizations and households defaulted on unequalled kinds of loans, and over five,000 companies declared monetary smash.

Hundreds of countless Americans were homeless and commenced accumulating in shanty organizations known as "Hoovervilles" that emerged all over the america.

President Hoover and Congress reacted through passing the Federal Home loan Bank Act, which aimed to inspire new home constructing and decrease foreclosure. The Emergency Situation Relief and Building And Construction Act (PERIOD), that included funding for public works efforts like as dams and the beginning of the Restoration Financing Corporation (RFC) in 1932, became the Hoover Administration's final try to beautify the economic machine. The Restoration Financing Corporation modified proper into a federal business employer with the functionality to loan as much as $2 billion to banks to preserve them and produce decrease lower lower back self-self guarantee in them. Having said that, $2 billion modified into inadequate to guard all the companies, and monetary company runs, and disasters continued. Quarter via place, the financial gadget weakened, with falling costs, profits, and artwork, fundamental to the political adjustment of 1932, which brought Franklin Delano Roosevelt to office. It is truly really worth maintaining in thoughts, too, that after volunteering failed, Hoover notion of thoughts that ended up being the form for additives of the New Offer.

Dry spell and disintegration conspired to create the Dust Bowl quick after President Franklin Delano Roosevelt took workplace in

1933, displacing numerous endless humans from their farms throughout the Midwest. Roosevelt promoted from the start that the financial gadget had to be reorganized at the manner to stay far from each other recession or expand the winning one. Through more federal government spending and the execution of economic reforms, New Offer initiatives aimed to supply want and deliver paintings and assist for the terrible.

The Emergency Situation Banking Act changed into signed into regulation inside the path of a five-day "monetary group holiday." It superior a shape for sound banks to resume underneath Treasury guidance, with federal funding effectively available if favored. The Securities Act of 1933 advanced an in depth regulative shape for the securities business corporation. The Securities Exchange Act of 1934, which advanced the Securities and Exchange Commission, observed. Both Acts' essential preparations are regardless of the truth that in effect, regardless of the fact that they have got been modified. The FDIC and the Glass-- Steagall Act both provided federal deposit coverage coverage.

The Agricultural Modification Act (AAA) offers monetary rewards for farmers to decrease manufacturing an terrific way to boom farming charges. The National Healing Administration (NRA) changed the American monetary device in some of procedures. It forced services to engage with the federal authorities to installation price codes thru the National Retail Association (NRA) if you want to combat deflationary "reduce-throat opposition" with the aid of the usage of developing minimum prices and incomes, exertions requirements, and aggressive situations in all markets. It supported tough paintings unions that might decorate wages, developing the going for walks beauty' obtaining energy. The NRA turn out to be brought unlawful with the resource of the usA. Supreme Court in 1935.

The First New Offer consists of those reforms and moreover a huge range of diverse comfort and rehab techniques. A new alphabet soup of corporations set up in 1933 and 1934, and moreover modern-day groups similar to the Restoration Financing Corporation, were used to try to stimulate the economic machine. By 1935, the "second New Offer" had delivered Social Security (which changed into later substantially broadened underneath the Fair Offer), a obligations software software for the out of work (the Works Development Administration, or WPA), and a major stimulant to the growth of difficult paintings unions through the National Labor Relations Board. Only three% of GDP was spent through the federal government in 1929. Under Hoover, the us financial debt as a portion of GDP extended from 20% to

40%. Roosevelt stored it at 40% until the war broke out, even as it leapt to 128%.

Other than for joblessness, which stayed excessive at eleven percent in 1936, but end up a long manner lower than the twenty-5 percentage rate decided in 1933, the other monetary indices had restored their levels of the late Nineteen Twenties. American industrial organization manufacturing went past that of 1929 in the spring of 1937 and stayed everyday till June 1937. In June 1937, the Roosevelt management attempted to stabilize the federal price range plan thru way of decreasing spending and raising taxes. The American monetary tool then had a severe recession that lasted for thirteen months, shielding the bulk of 1938. Within some months, industrial production reduced with the beneficial useful resource of over 30%, and resilient items manufacturing fell even quicker. Joblessness prolonged from 14.Three% in 1937 to 19.Zero% in 1938, with the amount of jobless rising from five million to extra than twelve million in early 1938. Production output visited 37% from its 1937 peak, going back to 1934 degrees.

Manufacturers lessen down on durable gadgets, and shares fell, in spite of the truth that personal revenue emerge as splendid 15% lower than it were in 1937. As joblessness skyrocketed, consumer spending fell, causing lots extra production lowerings. After June 1938, retail income started out out to upward push, work stepped forward, and commercial production multiplied. Following the restoration from the 1937-- 38 Great Depression, conservatives had the capability to set up a bipartisan conservative alliance to prevent destiny improvement of the New Offer, and at the same time as joblessness fell down to 2% in the early 1940s, they eliminated the WPA, CCC, and PWA alleviation packages. Social Security wasn't reversed.

Between 1933 and 1939, federal spending greater than tripled, prompting Roosevelt's critics to implicate him of changing America proper right right into a socialist country.

After the Second World War, the Great Depression turn out to be a top notch impact inside the adoption of social democracy and prepared economies in European global locations (see Marshall Plan). Till the Nineteen Seventies and 1980s, whilst Milton Friedman and other neoliberal monetary professionals developed and propagated the freshly created theories of neoliberalism and protected them into the Chicago School of Economics as an alternative method to the research look at of economics, Keynesianism stayed the most distinguished economic faculty in the US and components of Europe. Neoliberalism went on to project the Keynesian faculty of economics' supremacy in mainstream academic network and policymaking in the United States, accomplishing a peak of attraction with Ronald Reagan's election as President of the U.S. And Margaret Thatcher's election as Prime Minister of the U.K..

Chapter 10: Healing From The Great Depression

The recuperation from the Great Depression commenced in most international locations inside the route of the area in 1933. In the united states, recuperation started out in early 1933, but it took almost a whole decade to go back to 1929 GNP, and the joblessness price stayed over 15% in 1940, even though lower than the excessive of 25% in 1933.

Financial professionals disagree over what drove the united states' economic boom, which lasted for the a lot of Roosevelt's presidency (and the 1937 financial crisis that disrupted it). Most monetary professionals concur that Roosevelt's New Offer obligations each delivered on or accelerated the restoration, regardless of the truth that they had been in no manner ever aggressive sufficient to pull the monetary gadget out of economic disaster completely. Some monetary experts have additionally said the beneficial ramifications of Roosevelt's phrases and moves on forecasts of reflation and developing small fees of hobby.

The disruption of an monetary downturn that started out out out in late 1937 have become due to the turnaround of the precise equal reflationary efforts. The Banking Act of 1935, which efficiently improved reserve requirements, generating a monetary contraction that slowed the restoration, changed into one contributing insurance that reversed reflation. In 1938, the GDP started out to upward push all over again.

According to Christina Romer, the growth of the cash supply introduced approximately through large global gold inflows changed into a completely vital supply of the us monetary device's restoration, and the financial gadget placed out little indication of self-correction. The gold inflows were partially due to the dollar's devaluation and in element due to the degeneration of

Europe's political scenario. Milton Friedman and Anna J. Schwartz ascribed the restoration to monetary motives of their ebook A Monetary History of the united states, and stated that it became hindered appreciably via the Federal Reserve System's insufficient finance. Former Federal Reserve Chairman Ben Bernanke (2006-- 2014) said that financial elements to preserve in mind performed a big impact in every the worldwide economic crumble and superb recuperation. Bernanke additionally decided a massive function for institutional factors to hold in thoughts, in particular the restoring and reorganization of the monetary machine, and stressed the price of taking a check the Depression from an global mind-set.

Women's Contribution

Women's fantastic obligation modified into as homemakers; with out a normal glide of family earnings, dealing with meals, garments, and treatment ended up being notably extra hard. Kids had been not on time till families might also need to economically assist them, and birthrates reduced global. From 19.Three births in keeping with thousand population in 1930 to 17.Zero in 1935, the ordinary birthrate for fourteen widespread global locations reduced via 12%. In Canada, half of of Roman Catholic ladies disobeyed Church theories and used shipping manage to postpone their pregnancies.

Layoffs have been a great deal less ordinary in white-collar jobs a number of the few ladies inside the difficult paintings force, and they have been extra regular in slight enterprise markets. Nonetheless, there was large assist for restricting couples to at the least one paid interest, fearing that girls may lose their jobs if their spouses labored. Wives in the U.K. Had been little by little going into the tough work pressure, contending for issue-time jobs specifically.

Slow population development in France, specially in contrasted with Germany, stayed an immoderate trouble inside the Thirties. At the time of the Great Depression, there was an entire lot of resource for broadening properly-being offerings, especially for ladies within the circle of relatives. The Conseil Supérieur de l. A. Natalité lobbied for techniques inside the Code de la Famille (1939) that broadened federal government assist to families with kids and required corporations to hold dads' jobs, despite the fact that they had been immigrants.

Women extended their veggie gardens in rural and small-metropolis regions to encompass as plenty meals production as possible. Agricultural corporations within the U.S.A. Financed packages to educate homemakers a manner to enhance their gardens and grow chicken for meat and eggs. Feed sack dresses and unique merchandise were created with the useful aid of rural women for themselves, their family, and their houses out of feed sacks. African American women quiltmakers broadened their hobby in American towns, inspired partnership, and professional beginners. Quilts were produced for useful use from pretty quite a number low-cost substances, and they promoted social touch, friendship, and private pride amongst women.

Narrative information documents how homemakers in a contemporary-day industrial town dealt with cash and useful resource problems. They frequently upgraded strategies that their mothers used at the same time as they have been maturing in penniless households. Soups, beans, and noodles were used when you bear in mind that they have been plenty less highly-priced.

They bought the most inexpensive cuts of meat-- at instances even horse meat-- and made sandwiches and soups out of the

Sunday roast. They healed and guarded apparel, traded grown out of stuff with subsequent-door pals, and used cooler homes. The buy of latest domestic fixtures and gadgets turned into now not on time till a much better time. Most ladies moreover labored outside the residence or boarded with next-door associates, doing laundry for alternate or coins, and stitching for next-door buddies in exchange for some issue they will make a contribution. Additional food, greater areas, protection work, and cash loans had been utilized by prolonged families to help cousins and in-legal guidelines.

Main federal government coverage in Japan became deflationary, and it became the polar opposite of Keynesian fee. Subsequently, the federal government began an during the usa venture to encourage homes to lessen down on their usage, with a selected cope with spending thru the usage of ladies.

Under the Four-Year Plan of 1936, Germany's federal government tried to alter personal domestic consumption in order to advantage economic self-sufficiency. Economic self-sufficiency have become had to get prepared for and resource the approaching warfare, for that reason Nazi girls's organizations, specific propaganda agencies, and the kingdom all worked to mould such intake. Standard ideas of thrift and healthful living had been conjured up with the beneficial resource of the organizations, propaganda businesses, and government through mottos. Those efforts, even though, had been best partially effective in customizing homemakers' conduct.

The Second World War and Postwar Restoration

Economic chroniclers commonly concur that the Great Depression ended with the outbreak of The 2d international war. Most economic experts consider that federal government fee at the battle precipitated or extended the recuperation from the Great Depression, even though others revel in it carried out a bit effect inside the healing, even though it did assist to decrease joblessness.

In the years preceding as heaps as The second global warfare, rearmament strategies helped inside the stimulus of Europe's economies. Britain's joblessness charge has dropped to at least one.5 million through 1937. Following the start of battle in 1939, the mobilization of personnel placed an give up to joblessness.

When the usA. Got inside the battle in 1941, it in the end eliminated the ultimate vestiges of the Great Depression, bringing the joblessness price in the U.S.A. To ten%.

Huge army spending in the USA stepped forward financial improvement expenses, each camouflaging the outcomes of the Depression or efficiently completing it.

Regardless of the growing u . S . A . Money debt and brought taxes, businesspeople advanced their labor to growth output to benefit from profitable federal authorities agreements.

Chapter 11: The Last Rains

The final rains came gently, and they did no longer lessen the scarred earth. The plows crossed and re-crossed the rivulet marks. The last rains lifted the corn quickly and scattered the weed colonies and grass alongside the edges of the roads in order that the grey u . S . A . And the dark crimson u.S.A. Of the usa started out to vanish underneath a green cowl. In the very last a part of May the sky grew slight and the clouds that had hung in high puffs for goodbye within the spring had been dissipated. … The clouds appeared, and went away, and in some time they did now not strive any more. … The ground of the earth crusted, a skinny difficult crust, and due to the fact the sky have come to be light, so the earth have emerge as moderate, crimson in the crimson america and white within the grey u . S .." − John Steinbeck, The Grapes of Wrath

The Dust Bowl might in the long run be made viable via the manners wherein farmers planted flowers, but it's no longer as no matter the fact that the ones early farmers had been sincerely irresponsible either. As the us of a pushed west and settlers traveled at a few stage inside the frontier, they befell to be settling the land sooner or later of an surprisingly moist technology in information, and as a give up result, they constructed their farms in strategies that could limit the impact of the rain, not maximize it. Furthermore, maximum of the land being used belonged to ranchers who grazed their livestock at the acreage.

By 1900, however, an entire lot of the land have been so overgrazed to the aspect that it changed into beginning to erode, and Congress answered in 1904 with the useful resource of passing the Kinkaid Act, which gave 640 acres to every settler farming in western Nebraska. The rain started falling once more, making the place appear to be some thing but dry, and together with the passage of the Enlarged Homestead Act in 1909 – which gave every beginning farmer 320 acres to art work - a cutting-edge wave of settlers came from Europe to begin farms.

It have become inside the direction of this period that the foundation became surely laid for the Dust Bowl disaster. Those who came to to the American West advanced sure farming strategies that they surpassed at once to their children, and because of the fact the Russian Revolution and World War I drove up vegetable costs worldwide, those immigrants commenced farming even extra land the use of those equal techniques. Thus, even as the surprisingly wet length gave way to a drought in 1931, the second one-era farmers had been poorly appropriate to cope with the trade.

The nice component that stored many humans, as a minimum in the beginning, changed into that 1929 become an extraordinary 365 days agriculturally. Audrey Burdette of Valley Center, Kansas, remembered, "The 1929 harvest was a bumper crop in southwestern Kansas. Grain rolled into the grain boxes, placing a smile on every farmer's face. Soon acre after acre of pasture floor changed into have grow to be farmland with the rich, fertile loam ready to be planted. But nature is usually on pinnacle of things. The rains little by little have emerge as similarly and similarly apart. Time moved into the 30's and the middle states of the united states were in a drought."

The drought could were horrible at any time in records, however it was exacerbated by means of way of the monetary climate wherein it came about. The stock marketplace crash came at the heels of that bumper crop, crippling the American economic device and marked the start of the Great Depression. The ongoing economic troubles fueled a developing experience of panic and disaster that spread in the direction of the usa of the usa, leaving lasting impressions now not genuinely on personnel but furthermore at the more youthful. LeRoy Hankel recalled, "When the inventory market went proper right right down to now not something there was humans leaping out of -tale, three-tale houses in New York. That's what we heard except. Just jumping out! That changed into probably pretty a bit of a wonder. I turned into pretty younger at that point, but I nevertheless recollect the Crash. I expect probable word of mouth as plenty as analyzing it. Everything went to quantities, clearly right now! That's the way I preserve in mind it anyway. We simply didn't have no coins. It modified into, we had been in reality living off of the chickens and cows modified into what we have become doing."

Picture of a run on a economic institution in New York after the stock marketplace crash of 1929

As is frequently the case with monetary downturns, farmers have been hit the hardest. One man wrote, "Every day I scanned the sky, searching out symptoms and signs and symptoms and signs of the rain that could keep my wheat from ruin. One after some other, friends observed their vegetation reap a condition past preference of salvage." The few that had stored enough cash over the years to shop for more and more land all of sudden positioned that what they owned changed into nearly worthless. Carla Due remembered her parents' loss: "I recollect humans speakme. You understand that have end up everybody pointed out. I could not recognize a word they said…. But I suppose it emerge as all this, , everyone out of place their coins. It have become – My dad and mom have been so pleased that that they had provided the farm in advance than. So, they took their cash and that they had paid $10,000 at the farm, half of of of what the farm price. It price them $20,000. And I notion, nicely, now wait a minute. By the time we moved on the farm, it wasn't definitely properly worth what we nevertheless owed on it. So, it regarded to me like they out of place their coins, however I did no longer say some thing. Because it without a doubt wasn't in reality really worth what we, by the point we moved on the farm, the early 30s, everything went down. You understand, you may buy eighty acres for $three,000."

Picture of a cotton farm inside the 1930s

The Wind Grew Stronger

The wind grew more potent, whisked below stones, carried up straws and antique leaves, or even little clouds, marking its direction as it sailed for the duration of the fields. The air and the sky darkened and via them the solar shone redly, and there has been a uncooked sting within the air. During a night time the wind raced faster over the land, dug cunningly some of the rootlets of the corn, and the corn fought the wind with its weakened leaves until the roots have been freed thru using the prying wind after which each stalk settled wearily sideways closer to the earth and pointed the course of the wind. The sunrise got here, but no day. In the gray sky a pink sun appeared, a dim purple circle that gave a touch moderate, like nightfall; and as that day superior, the dusk slipped once more inside the direction of darkness, and the wind

cried and whimpered over the fallen corn."
– John Steinbeck, The Grapes of Wrath

Due to their dependence at the land, Midwestern farmers bore the brunt of the struggling due to the Great Depression. Those who grew plant life and raised cattle on the coasts have been better off thinking about that they did no longer have to take care of drought situations normally, but for those alongside the wheat belt, the "Dirty 1930s" have become absolutely devastating. Congressman Clifford R. Hope later positioned, "None of the calamity periods can test from the mind-set of monetary loss, long lasting distress, suffering, and discouragement with the decade of the Thirties. The Great Depression ... affected Kansas clearly because it did every one-of-a-kind a part of the us, however ... Kansas and the neighboring Great Plains states had been given a double dose of misery and calamity."

Indeed, most people who lived thru one in no way forgot what a dirt hurricane was like. Audrey Burdette certainly never did: "Mother and Dr. Broady had made arrangements for Ned to have a remedy that afternoon and Don, my greater youthful brother, drove. They hadn't been long past however a few minutes when Dad observed a lower returned line at the horizon off to the northwest. He watched! Another dust storm become at the circulate and it have become coming within the direction people speedy. By the time the storm clouds have been darkening over our domestic we knew someplace on the road to town a very younger the usage of pressure changed into responsible for the family car and its occupants. We have been involved for them. Dad desired the rest of the own family to go to the storm cellar, however if I undergo in thoughts successfully, my youngest sister, Iola, and I had been the only one to make the trek down those stairs. And we did now not live inside the cellar very prolonged. Although it modified into black as night time time, Dad in no way stopped scanning the street for a glimpse of the returning car. Hours exceeded, the hurricane lightened, after which vehicle lighting were seen as despite the truth that coming via a fog. They had stopped on the road in the blackness after which slowly inched their manner to a farmhouse for secure haven."

Though many of the states inside the Southwest were affected, those dwelling in Kansas had been most of the worst patients. After all, it wasn't simply the dirt that made the Dust Bowl but moreover the wind, and Kansas had lots of every, as Burdette cited: "Southwestern Kansas is an area that enjoys winds and they introduced approximately the region to end up a dirt bowl. Dry loose soil sifted from one farm to every exceptional. If the wind blew from the north, we jokingly blamed the dust typhoon on Nebraska. The black dust sifted everywhere. When the wind blew from the south, we jokingly remarked approximately the pink Oklahoma dust. But it have grow to be not humorous! It have grow to be extreme. The dust storms would possibly blow in so speedy. You couldn't understand one turn out to be coming till you observed the black rolling clouds of dirt billowing higher and better in the distance."

Chapter 12: A Photograph Of Dirt Piling Up In The Direction Of A Barn In Kansas

1931 marked the start of the important dry durations. The soil within the Midwestern states and the Southern Plains have turn out to be so dry that it modified proper right into a sort of black dirt, ensuring that whenever the wind kicked up, it would create a dirt typhoon. The farming families which have been familiar with the horrible wintry climate snowstorms that swept at a few stage inside the prairies each wintry weather referred to as these dirty windstorms "black blizzards," and they had been as quick as defined by using the use of manner of a Kansas wheat farmer named Lawrence Svobida in his memoirs, Farming the Dust Bowl: "At different times a cloud is seen to be drawing close to from a distance of many miles. Already it has the banked look of a cumulus cloud, but it is black in preference to white and it hangs low, seeming to hug the earth. Instead of being sluggish to alternate its form, it seems to be rolling on itself from the crest downward. As it sweeps onward, the landscape is grade by grade blotted out. Birds fly in terror in advance than the storm, and simplest the ones which is probably strong of wing can also additionally additionally escape. The smaller birds fly until they may be exhausted, then fall to the ground, to proportion the future of the heaps of jack rabbits which perish from suffocation."

Picture of a black snowstorm in Liberal, Kansas

Picture of a black snow fall in Rolla, Kansas in 1935

A 1934 picture of a black snowfall in South Dakota

Grace Brooks, who grew up in Wichita, Kansas, recalled her first enjoy with the phenomenon: "It have end up Palm Sunday and my circle of relatives were to church. After lunch, the day have become so wonderful that my eighty-9 year antique grandfather decided to take an afternoon walk. The temperature rose to 80 four levels. While he come to be out walking there regarded on the northwest horizon a cloud that gave the impression of a black snow fall. The swirling black dirt clouds had been rolling in the direction of the farm at an superb tempo of about 38 miles in step with hour! It were calm just in advance than the wind and dirt hit the farm approximately 3:00 p.M. The circle of relatives have become amazed thru how fast it occurred. The temperature dropped hastily to 50 ranges. Very brief the solar was blocked out and it changed into pitch black. We couldn't see our fingers in the the the front of our faces."

The stage of darkness professional in the direction of those storms turn out to be identical to that professional through groups following a volcanic eruption. One man wrote, "So the Dust Bowl had taught us every other lesson; specifically, that bare floor exposed to the solar will remodel heat breezes into fiery blasts. The warm wind appeared to rob all plant life of its energy. This modified into my first revel in of a wind that added on my face to blister so that the skin peeled off." Indeed, the ones caught outside in such conditions located themselves in grave chance, as Brooks defined: "Suddenly, the circle of relatives discovered out there was an emergency due to the fact grandpa had now not lower back from his stroll. Although I have turn out to be quality 5 years vintage I recollect our circle of relatives placing moist rags over our faces and going out into the choking dirt to discover grandpa. The dirt end up gritty in our eyes. We cautiously stayed at the course many of the house and the fowl house, which turned into best a quick distance north of the antique residence and started taking turns yelling GRANDPA, GRANDPA. After the hurricane have end up a awesome deal less fierce grandpa modified into located. It changed right into a delight to see him arrive domestic. The own family have turn out to be worried approximately his fitness because of the amount of dust he inhaled. While strolling alongside the barbed cord fence he reduce his hands and the swirling dirt created static strength in the cord that shocked him. However, Grandpa recovered fast from all of the dust he took into his lungs. He short modified into again to telling his exquisite memories. As Arlene wrote, 'Grandpa modified right into a survivor.'"

Picture of a person in the center of a dirt storm

There Was No Break

The human beings came out of their homes and smelled the new stinging air and included their noses from it. And the youngsters came out of the houses, however they did not run or shout as they might have completed after a rain. Men stood through their fences and checked out the ruined corn, drying speedy now…The men have been silent and they did no longer flow into frequently. And the women got here out of the houses to stand through their men—to feel whether or not or no longer this time the men might damage. … The kids stood with the aid of way of, drawing figures within the dust with bare feet … to appearance whether or not or no longer or no longer women and men could break. … After some time the faces of the searching men … have come to be difficult and angry and resistant. Then the girls knew that they have been stable and there was no break." – John Steinbeck, The Grapes of Wrath

The following yr, in 1932, the dust storms extended in every wide variety and depth, as people who saved music of such occasions recorded 14 dust storms in 1932 and extra than twice that many in 1933. By this time, the Great Depression had a stranglehold on the United States and plenty of the sector, so even people who had as soon as been wealthy were feeling the pinch of poverty. There have become a sharp boom internal the quantity of suicides in the kingdom, even amongst farmers, a tough and fast formerly believed to be too difficult and self-enough to hotel to such measures. Elroy Hoffman stated the outcomes of one dirt hurricane: "[I]t modified into horrible. I apprehend, when I started out out farming I sowed alfalfa south of the residence a protracted manner, and plowed the floor brilliant and clean, . And my partner had simply wiped easy residence. And a hell of a dirt hurricane rise up, and also you want to have seen our residence. It in fact made her ill, . It even blew seed out of the floor."

Farmers were now not the best ones affected, due to the truth all of us who had to do any type of organisation in the path of that era come to be suffering from the storms. Filled with despair, human beings commenced to give up and take delivery of that they needed to circulate without delay to someplace new. One guy described, "With my monetary belongings at last exhausted and my fitness critically, if not absolutely impaired, I am at very last organized to surrender and depart the Dust Bowl all of the time. With teens and ambition ground into the very dust itself, I can best go together with the flow with the tide."

Even individuals who were very young inside the path of the "Dirty 1930s" had been privy to all that transpired manner to reminiscences informed to them via way in their elders. One lady wrote of the instances, "I grow to be born in 1933, so I don't have any memory of the dirt storms. However, I do remember my mother and father speakme approximately them. They stated they'll wet rags to stuff across the house windows and however in the morning they had to sweep the residence out. My mother said she may also want to wet tea towels and drape them over my crib at the same time as she positioned me to mattress at night time. In the morning you may see the outline of my frame at the crib sheets. My father worked for the Chevrolet dealership, which emerge as about four blocks from our house. My dad may additionally need to stroll domestic for lunch every day. One dust hurricane day he known as mother to inform her he changed into on his manner home. She located a lamp inside the window to help guide him to the house. He walked into the facet of the house earlier than he knew he become there."

By the time President Franklin D. Roosevelt have become inaugurated in 1933, the usa changed into in dire straits. Banks had closed, taking with them the difficult-earned financial savings of farmers and one-of-a-type on foot guys, however the bankers had been no longer actually at fault each; they could not have expected that their investments might fail any greater than the farmers must have anticipated that their land may dry up and not produce its plants. The bankers believed prosperity ought to final for all time, on the identical time as the farmers believed the same have become proper of rain and sunshine. The early part of the ultimate decade proved every companies incorrect, and now they have been in search of to the government for a solution.

Fortunately, Roosevelt have become as an lousy lot as the assignment, and he short have become the hero of the going for walks man. After retaining a four-day lengthy economic institution excursion, the president labored with Congress to pass the Emergency Banking Act, law that furnished safety for destiny economic group deposits and endorsed human beings to just accept as proper with the neighborhood banks all over again. Likewise, the Emergency Farm

Mortgage Act and the Farm Credit Act, moreover passed in 1933, provided a way for operating men to preserve their farms and keep away from foreclosures. However, it modified into nonetheless an open query to many whether or not the farms were even sincerely nicely worth keeping. Harvey Pickrel described, "We went down, I anticipate it modified into Great Bend, Kansas, and the character says, 'I'll sell you a four wheel Go-Dig, however it is out in that undertaking available.' And he stated, 'About all you could see is the pinnacle of it.' He says, 'The rest is drifted below dust.' We had to dig that out. He offered it to us for almost nothing, but we needed to dig that thing out of the dirt because it had drifted in round it. And he said, 'We do not use it anymore, we can't decorate corn. It's too dry.' ... I keep in mind I became out working the sphere inside the future, and we had the ones tumbleweeds which you'd name them. You possibly recognize what those are. Well, they had been rolled up inside the course of my north fence. And I grow to be walking, and — the posts simply were rotten and it had woven cord up towards it — and proper right here that whole fence virtually come turning over, over, over, over, finishing. It blew that fence 1 / four of a mile with the ones weeds against it. It have become an lousy venture to choose it up. All you could do became placed it in a sell off some area as it grow to be no longer usable anymore."

Pickrel similarly described just how excessive the dirt accrued in sure areas: "Well, I can don't forget numerous humans that out of place their farms. When topics have been rich, they had been capable of bypass. When prices came down, why, obviously they could not finance their debt anymore. See, I can maintain in thoughts within the early 30s, the charge of corn had been given so low that we have been burning ear corn in our heating stoves in region of coal … But, the person advised us approximately him coming domestic from town at some point and he stated, 'The dust blew so lousy I could not see my personal driveway and abruptly I heard some element below the car. I got out to appearance what it changed into and I'd run over my very personal mailbox.' He says, 'You virtually couldn't see a detail.' Well, those who stayed, an entire lot of them left the us of a of course. From proper here, looks as if an entire lot of humans from here went to Oregon. But folks that stayed, why they completed pretty properly, some of them."

Chapter 13: A Photograph Of Buried Machinery In Dallas, South Dakota

On Relief

"We're sorry, stated the proprietor guy. The economic organization, the fifty-thousand-acre proprietor can't be responsible. You're on land that isn't yours. Once over the road possibly you can pick cotton in the fall. Maybe you may skip on comfort. Why don't you pass on west to California? There's art work there, and it in no manner gets cold. Why, you could attain out everywhere and pick out an orange. Why, there's constantly some form of crop to work in. Why don't you flow there?" – John Steinbeck, The Grapes of Wrath

A picture of eroded farmland due to the Dust Bowl

In June 1933, as the summer season modified into yet again heating up, the primary Civilian Conservation Corps camp committed to stopping soil erosion opened in Alabama, and through the stop of the summer season, there had been 161 similar camps throughout the u . S .. Not simplest did the CCC beautify the quality of the farmland by means of the usage of slowing or on occasion even preventing erosion, it additionally supplied jobs for those disregarded of exertions at the equal time because the farmers could not manage to pay for to plant a crop. Carla Due recalled, "Oh, certain. There were some of the younger fellows inside the community. They positive did [join the CCC enthusiastically]. What have been they going to do? They could not get a job. They could not make a penny everywhere. They have been genuinely happy there has been this sort of component they will flow into into...They did now not take the cash and go and characteristic fun with it. They had been given $five.00 and the relaxation went to their families, their dad and mom or some thing, who have been looking it. And it became superb the rescue of pretty a few families."

Delbert Apetz have emerge as one of these "younger fellows" who joined the CCC, and he later remembered, "I left right right right here in York, went to Hebron. That end up the induction station. From Hebron I went to Pawnee City and in Pawnee City, this is in which we stayed. I turned into right there on the fairgrounds. There changed into barracks and the whole thing made there. And what we done – the farmer, all he performed modified into paid for the fence posts and barbwire. We need to located it up for him. ... There, you went out on the farms and dug in fence posts and stuff like that. It changed into hard paintings. ... No, it genuinely is – it have end up difficult art work. But no character seemed to bitch down there, because of the reality you had an area to sleep, a place to devour – which changed into quite skimpy pretty some times at domestic. So, no, I in no way complained approximately it."

American farmers have constantly been unbiased with the resource of nature and manner of existence, such a whole lot of had a problem accepting help or perhaps advice from the authorities. As such, folks that stored a long way from government alleviation was hoping or perception that they'll live at the disaster on their very very own at the same time as no longer having to attain out to Washington. However, it rapid have emerge as apparent that the situation have become too excessive for any character to address by myself. For instance, people couldn't provide you with the coins for to shop for the quantity of red meat the American farmers have been producing, some difficulty LeRoy Hankel remembered years later: "Bill Camps turn out to be my uncle. And inside the '30s, he end up a quite suitable hog guy. And even as the drought years came, he stop, quite an awful lot, raising them hogs. But, he did have about 12, 13 shoats [that] weighed a hundred pounds. ... He took them to Hampton. [They] weighed about a hundred pounds, and they shipped them into Omaha. And after all of the freight invoice and the whole thing, fee turn out to be paid, he got one dollar bill from them shoats. That's all of the coins he were given. And he knowledgeable me, he said, 'I do not recognize why I cashed that test. I want I'd [have] framed it!' But, he had, all those shoats weighed one hundred kilos, and one greenback bill is all he got for them hogs. Hogs had been spherical three cents a pound."

In hopes of raising the costs charged for cattle and special commodities, Congress set up the Agricultural Adjustment Administration, and the plan modified into for the AAA to paintings with farmers to plant the proper plants and stabilize costs. Some resisted the concept, but as LeRoy Hankel pointed out, "Most of them went [into the program]. There have grow to be just a few that could no longer have some thing to do with it. But, the majority of people, all of them went into this system... There's some that stated, 'The authorities is not going to tell me what to do.' There end up a number of them. Now, I do not assume there has been too many. They did now not need the authorities to inform them what to do. That's the entire story. You needed to abide with the useful resource of using their pointers. If you had to depart 10 acres out, they came out and measured it, and checked it, and checked you out."

Although the concept of leaving land fallow can also moreover have grated on many people's nerves, a comparable huge fashion of human beings have been outraged at the same time as the AAA ordered the slaughter of more than 6 million shoats (younger pigs). While this did stress the price of meat all over again up, it additionally introduced approximately a public outcry in opposition to the waste, and it couldn't be denied that throwing meat away while Americans starved regarded preposterous. In response, the authorities set up the Federal Surplus Relief Corporation, which allotted the food the authorities supplied from the farmers to needy clients. Everything from apples and beans to cotton for apparel might also fast face government law.

West to California

In the little homes the tenant humans sifted their assets and the property of their fathers and of their grandfathers. Picked over their possessions for the adventure to the west. The men have been ruthless because of the truth the past have been spoiled, however the ladies knew how the beyond may cry to them within the coming days. ... They walked again to the farms, arms in wallet, and heads down, shoes kicking the pink dust up. Maybe we are able to start all yet again, within the new wealthy land—in California, in which the fruit grows. We'll start over." — John Steinbeck, The Grapes of Wrath

Dorothea Lange's photo of a migrant mom who traveled from Texas to California to pick out peas

As the Dust Bowl persisted to wreak havoc, individuals who gave in desired an opportunity, and their picks would possibly have in addition political effects. Many farmers who gave up on farming inside the Midwest or who out of place their farms to the monetary organization determined to go to California to searching for their fortunes, in issue because of the reality they heard there was some component of an agricultural increase taking vicinity at the West Coast. The hassle, of direction, grow to be that even as there has been hundreds of labor for the guys already there, there has been no longer enough art work to help each family that traveled to the dominion searching out a contemporary day home, or at least a place to stay on the disaster they placed themselves in.

Florence Thompson, who would end up the face of the Dust Bowl generation, left for California some years in advance than most, but thru 1931 she turned into managing the identical worrying situations everybody else end up. She explained, "I left Oklahoma in 1925 and went to Oroville [California]. That's wherein them 3 women' dad died, in Oroville, 1931. And I changed into 28 years vintage and I had 5...It have become very hard. And cheap. I picked cotton in Firebaugh, while that female there was about years antique, I picked cotton in Firebaugh for fifty-cents a hundred [pounds]. I normally picked around 450, 500. I failed to even weigh a hundred pounds. I lived down there in Shafter, and I'd leave home earlier than daylight and are to be had after darkish. We absolutely existed! Anyway, we lived. We survived, permit's placed it that manner. I walked from what they referred to as a Hoover camp ground right there at the bridge [in Bakersfield], I walked from there to way down on First Street, and worked at a Penny A Dish [kitchen] down there for fifty-cents an afternoon and the leftovers. Yeah, they offer me what come to be left over to take home with me. Sometimes, I'd supply home water buckets full."

Thompson went on to talk about her well-known image and the manner it came to be taken: "Well, [in 1936] we started out out from L.A. To Watsonville. And the timing chain broke on my vehicle. And I had a person to drag into this pea camp in Nipomo. I began to prepare dinner dinner for my children, and all of the little youngsters across the camp got here in. 'Can I virtually have a bite? Can I truely have a bit?' And they modified into hungry, them people became. And I were given my automobile constant, and I become truely on the brink of pull out at the same time as she [famous photographer Dorothea Lange] come lower again and snapped my image."

Dorothea Lange's well-known photograph of Florence Thompson and her children have become captioned, "Destitute pea pickers in California. Mother of 7 youngsters. Age thirty-. Nipomo, California."

A picture of migrant people residing in a squatter camp in California

Though it is straightforward to be sympathetic with the plight of ladies and men like Thompson, their presence inside the usa did result in a sure amount of civil unrest, as too many humans started vying for too few jobs. Violence broke out whilst extra than 18,000 people of the Cannery and Agricultural Workers Industrial Union went on strike for twenty-4 days. During the riots that regularly broke out even as a person attempted to pass the timber line, loads of people were injured and 3 killed. However, even as it ended, the union had scored recognition through maximum big-scale growers in California, in addition to a sizable growth in what they have been paid.

Furthermore, even the risk of violence did no longer preserve humans away, as many felt that that they had no choice but to get to a higher weather except. Lawrence Svobida explained, "The medical doctors of our vicinity recognize that dust endangers the life of all of us whose health is impaired from illness, and that it's miles often the direct cause of the deaths of human beings formerly robust and healthy. There are many sufferers who in no way go to a health center; and many patients who're taken there at ultimate with the useful resource of loved ones are moribund even as admitted, and die indoors some hours."

The risk to their fitness, and that in their children, is what drove many humans on. Still, Svobida decided the sight of such a whole lot of humans pulling out demanding: "Most farmers, once they determine to leave their farms, load their family possessions in automobiles or trailers, and take to the highway below electricity. Many of the townspeople, having no approach of shipping, are forced to desolate tract their belongings and go away walking, with great the garments on their backs and such bundles as can be carried of their palms. After each hurricane the highways are thronged with those refugees. On the roads on foot thru Meade and Montezuma I genuinely have visible loads of human beings in infinite procession, heading out of the Dust Bowl. So it modified into in 1934, in 1935, in 1936, in 1937, and in 1938—masses of households deserting towns and farms, all looking for a few haven of consolation from the dust."

Meanwhile, topics went from bad to worse for those nonetheless within the Midwest. In the late spring of 1934, the harm finished thru the Dust Bowl grew exponentially, gobbling up increasingly of the region, and it grow to be now clean that the United States changed into inside the middle of the worst drought in its statistics. By the cease of May, more than seventy five% of the united states of a had been affected, and 27 states had been near disintegrate. LeRoy Hankel later recalled, "Boy we had dust right here. And you couldn't keep a house easy or some thing. Dust all of the time. We had a sprinkle - I do no longer are aware about it emerge as April or May, and I passed off to be in Seward. And virtually the manner the drops fell down on the sidewalk, they modified into all scattered spherical there, and it clearly depart a touch puddle of dirt right round honestly that drop. It end up definitely — Everything modified into protected with dirt. That's the way that '34 [was]. To me, '34 modified into in all likelihood the worst drought one year that we had within the complete bunch. The unique years appeared like within the spring you'll get only a rain or . It might make the primary crop of hay and get corn and everything started out. And even some years it emerge as a touch bit moist. And then the corn did upward push up. It grow to be beginning to tassel. I maintain in mind we changed into coming domestic within the combine. We'd simply had been given thru combining. Our corn come to be up over our heads and it seemed real. And approximately three, 4 days [after] it modified into – we already knew that we misplaced it. It clearly were given warm and the corn actually dried right off."

Dorothea Lange's image of a Missouri female who traveled to California

This Dorothea Lange photograph of youngsters from Oklahoma who have traveled to California changed into captioned, "Children of Oklahoma drought refugees on toll road close to Bakersfield, California. Family of six; no steady haven, no food, no cash and nearly no gasoline. The toddler has bone tuberculosis."

Chapter 14: The Bank Or The Company

"Some of the proprietor guys have been kind because of the fact they hated what they had to do, and a number of them were angry due to the fact they hated to be cruel, and a number of them had been cold because of the fact that they had long within the past placed that one could not be an proprietor except one were bloodless. And they all were stuck in something large than themselves. Some of them hated the arithmetic that drove them, and some were afraid, and a few worshiped the mathematics because it supplied a safe haven from idea and from feeling. If a economic organization or a finance enterprise owned the land, the proprietor guy said, The Bank—or the Company—goals—needs—insists—have to have—as even though the Bank or the Company have been a monster, with concept and feeling, which had ensnared them." – John Steinbeck, The Grapes of Wrath

In June 1934, President Roosevelt signed into law the Taylor Grazing Act, which gave the USA permission to fence off a hundred and forty million acres of land that it owned inside the Midwest and rent it to ranchers on a carefully monitored foundation. Unfortunately, the act proved to be too little too overdue, for at the same time as the authorities have become capable of forestall the land from persevering with to be overused, it could not restore the damage finished in a unmarried day. In truth, even the federal government could not preserve the already overused and scarred earth from blowing away. LeRoy Hankel defined one of the dirt storms from that 12 months: "Everything emerge as grimy you recognize, with dust blowing all through. And then in '34 whilst the dirt storms started out from the west at North Platte come to be what I have become knowledgeable. And I'll inform you that seemed just like the worst hurricane you ever discovered. It changed into best a cloud coming proper over, that is what it appeared. And it have become all black. I've heard as masses as a hundred mile consistent with hour wind. I do not know if it changed into that strong. Myself, I don't think it changed into. But a automobile stopped at Frazier's. He emerge as using earlier of it. He said, 'You recognize, that typhoon started in the back of me about North Platte.' And he said, 'I outrun it until here.' And he stated, 'I virtually had to stop.' But the entire sky within the west, as far as you – only a black cloud. That's the way it seemed. But it turn out to be all dirt and that is all we have been given out of it. We have been given all dirt. Dave Frazier had his truck sitting out within the the front of the shop there and it even blew that approximately 30-40 toes – definitely right down the road."

One of the most crucial dangers going via the common farmer at a few stage in the Dust Bowl became the threat of losing the farm. Farming have turn out to be a debtor's agency, that means farmers typically mortgaged their houses to live at the iciness, with the aim of paying off the loan the subsequent summer time whilst subsequent 12 months's vegetation, that would in fact be higher, got here in. The banks and the loan corporations understood this and had been capable of deliver some mortgages as long as there had been now not too numerous them and as long as the payments can be stored up. Thus, even as the plants failed in 1931, it changed into intense however now not an emergency. However, it have end up greater excessive in 1932 and 1933, and through the use of the usage of 1934, the banks themselves came to the perception that they've been no longer going to get their investors' coins again. When that scenario arose, they frequently felt they had no choice but to foreclose.

Harvey Pickrel modified into one of the fortunate ones: "If I don't forget proper, I owed $four hundred on it [the tractor] and simply at some stage in the street over here is the person who I supplied it from. I come into this financial institution proper right here [Cornerstone Bank] and that they had an antique boy that become working for them. And he checked out my phrase that'd come due, and he stated, 'You are not simply properly worth this, what's on this look at.' He says, 'I can't mortgage you any cash. You've have been given to decide a few manner, we are going to want to sell you out or some thing.'

Well, it failed to make me satisfied. I stated, 'Well, I do not realize approximately that. The simplest thing I realize, I'm sincere and I'll pay it.' And I went to depart the bank, and the individual that owned this financial institution ... he met me on the door. And he stated, 'Harvey, you're mad. What's the problem?' And I advised him. He took me lower again in and he observe the pedigree to this vintage boy. He stated, 'Don't you recognise this is our industrial employer of the next day? You're walking [him] away.' He said, 'You address these more youthful boys like this.' So, I were given my word renewed."

For those an awful lot less lucky, the federal government surpassed the Frazier-Lemke Farm Bankruptcy Act in 1934, restricting the circumstance underneath which a economic group may additionally want to foreclose and as a result making it tons much less complicated for farmers to hold their land. It first expired in 1938 however changed into renewed again and again till the rich years following the cease of World War II.

For folks who could not be helped by that law, they have been often able to keep away from the perceived shame of foreclosure by using way of promoting their farms to someone else. This might also need to expose to be useful to both events, for the motive that seller were given some cash out of the transaction and the customer were given a bargain. In truth, that is how Louise Dougherty were given her first home: "Yes. The house that we moved into, in which we lived the primary few years we have been married, the humans have been going to lose. And so some constructing and mortgage contacted John, my husband, and stated, 'If you'll go with the glide in and pay the rest [of the mortgage] off then we can not foreclose. And so the human beings that were living there moved out, left the furnishings. I propose, they moved into a bit apartment downtown, and John and I moved into that residence and he paid his hire there."

Dougherty's scenario confirmed that regardless of how terrible the Dust Bowl got, some human beings want to find out a silver lining, a sentiment echoed by using the usage of one housewife who weathered the Kansas Dust Bowl: "Strange as it could seem, we had fun. I can endure in mind the days whilst the wind and dirt could probable blow till about sundown. When the wind might circulate down and the air would clear. One of the pals must drive into the outside…and say 'come over for supper'. We would hurriedly healing a dish of some element to take and the whole own family may fit; after supper we'd play playing playing cards and certainly have an outstanding time. We additionally had birthday party dances in our homes; there might be or 3 men to be had who achieved a violin and a guitar; we'd pass enough furnishings out of the living room so we might have enough room to bop…Most parents controlled to shop for a radio, which changed into a few element new, and we spent many a night taking note of programs and tune."

Chapter 15: The Dust Came In So Thinly

When the night time time time came again it became black night time time, for the celebrities could not pierce the dust to get down, and the window lighting fixtures could not even unfold beyond their very very own yards. Now the dirt modified into calmly combined with the air, an emulsion of dust and air. Houses were shut tight, and material wedged spherical doorways and home home home windows, however the dirt got here in so thinly that it couldn't be seen in the air, and it settled like pollen at the chairs and tables, at the dishes. The humans brushed it from their shoulders. Little traces of dirt lay on the door sills." – John Steinbeck, The Grapes of Wrath

In spite of the exquisite spin that some people were capable of located on their occasions, instances had been however hard, and they had been most effective getting greater difficult as 1934 got here to an prevent. By that point, in keeping with one deliver, 35 million previously cultivated acres had been laying fallow, a hundred million acres had no topsoil left, and 100 twenty five million acres of land had been in hazard of losing their topsoil. These grim facts compelled the government to create the Drought Relief Service in 1935. Their first order of enterprise enterprise company grow to be to buy up herds of ravenous farm animals at an average price of $16 in keeping with head. The government then destroyed those that have been in too poor a condition to be butchered and gave the rest to the FSRC to be killed and processed for distribution to needy households in the route of the u . S .. As someone later wrote, "The authorities livestock buying software program modified into a God-send to many farmers, as they could not manipulate to pay for to preserve their livestock, and the authorities paid a better rate than they'll advantage in neighborhood markets."

At the equal time the government was studying a way to address the storms and the monetary fallout, close by households also had been getting a sense for the uncommon sensations that each new dirt storm added about. Timothy Egan recalled, "One of the subjects that passed off truely earlier than a duster hit modified into there has been this splendid static power within the air. And so humans used to hold a sequence in their automobile to ground the power. So you failed to pressure everywhere while now not having this chain that you'd then throw out and drag it alongside the floor to floor the strength purpose your radio may also want to exit, your electric powered stuff have to brief. And anybody ought to speak about the manner you actually could not shake a few different man or woman's hand in advance than this type of dusters purpose the static have become so strong. It become the kinetic power that changed into in the air definitely before a duster hit."

In April 1935, Congress accepted the Emergency Relief Appropriation Act, which earmarked $525 million for farmers struggling monetary hardships because of the drought. This coins modified into desperately preferred, as increasingly humans had been dropping their houses and livelihoods to the wind, the dirt, and the banks.

While this modified proper right into a boon to the ones inside the Dust Bowl, it changed into in huge factor overshadowed via the opportunity regulation that went into effect that equal day and installation the Works Progress Administration. Before it became abolished at the stop of the Depression, the WPA would possibly hire greater than eight.Five million Americans, however Stan Jensen later shared that, at the same time as they desired the work, it changed into difficult on many guys's delight to artwork for the WPA: "Most of the farmers, pretty lots they all, while the WPA got here in, worked at the roads. I think, as I don't forget, they were given a dollar an afternoon for running. And in the event that they had a set of horses, they have been given a further 50-cents an afternoon for the horses. My dad never did that. He absolutely in no way did that. I do now not realize how he made it, but he did. He modified right into a pretty independent guy, and proud. I expect there was masses of delight in that, not having to do this."

www.ingramcontent.com/pod-product-compliance
Lightning Source LLC
Chambersburg PA
CBHW071447080526
44587CB00014B/2026